A

LEADERSHIP

DEVELOPMENT

Workbook

Biblical Principles on Leadership

STEVE FITZPATRICK

A

LEADERSHIP

DEVELOPMENT

WORKBOOK

Biblical Principles on Leadership

Steve Fitzpatrick

Copyright © 2015 by Steve Fitzpatrick

ISBN 978-1-61529-163-2

Vison Publishing
1115 D Street
Ramona, CA 92065
www.booksbyvision.com

Table of Contents

PREFACE

This workbook has been a lifetime in development. I have taken topics that I have taught, preached and developed in seminars around the world and compiled them in this format. A few years ago I was just finishing a seminar with Pastor Aguayo in Lima, Peru when he said to me, "Why don't you put this material into a book format and I will help you get it into print." After publishing this book first in Spanish, this new and edited version is finally in English.

For years I have been training pastoral leaders and strengthening local churches in over 40 countries. I can clearly see that God is moving around the world. In country after country the church is growing with new believers. Currently someone is being birthed into the Kingdom of God at a rate of one every two seconds. Praise God for that is truly miraculous. But with the growth of new believers in the Kingdom there is also a corresponding problem that must be addressed.

A few years ago I was heading to one of my seminars being held in Argentina. I was travelling in a taxi with Pastor Gonzalez when I casually asked, "So, what's been going on in your ministry lately?" To which he responded, "Oh, last week we just opened another church in a nearby town." So I asked him, "Wow that's great, so how many churches have you opened altogether?" Amazingly he said, "Praise God that was the 200th church we've started!" I was astounded, and I guess my dropped jaw told him so. "But, Steve," he said, "you've got to realize that this is what the Holy Spirit is currently doing throughout Latin America. Where in years past we suffered great persecution, and getting people saved was so very difficult, now that has changed. I have the faith today that I can go to any town, start preaching on a street corner, and in a matter of two weeks birth a church. Starting churches seems to be the easy part, the difficulty is in developing the leaders to shepherd those churches. And that is why I am so thankful for your efforts. We need help in training leaders!"

I have come to realize that the training of leaders needs to cover three basic areas; character, conduct and content. **Character** is who you are. **Conduct** is how you function in your ministry. And **Content** is what you believe. If you, as a leader, can have basic training in each of these areas then you will be much better prepared to serve the Lord in the ministry to which you have been called.

With these thoughts in mind I have prepared the following material in a **catechismal format**. For centuries this format has been used to educate students. Catechism is simply instruction through the use of questions and answers. With a catechism format this book can then be used by an individual for personal study, by a group with an informal leader, or in a classroom setting with a formal instructor. Unless otherwise stated all scripture references will be from the New International Version. However you choose to use this workbook I trust that you will be blessed and further established in your faith and leadership gifting.

Steve Fitzpatrick

Section 1

CHARACTER
Who you are…

CHARACTER – WHO YOU ARE

DEFINING CHARACTER

1. **In what ways can Character be defined?**

   a. **Romans 5:3-4** - *Not only so, but we also rejoice in our sufferings, because we know that suffering produces perseverance; perseverance, character; and character, hope.*

      i. Character is the translation of the Greek word, *dokime*. This is defined as to test, to value after 'assayal' (or the value established after the refining process has taken place).

      ii. NAS simply translates it, *proven character*.

      iii. Notice how character is developed in context. Suffering produces perseverance and perseverance produces character.

         - Suffering = (Grk.) to crowd, to pressure, to rub

         - Perseverance = (Grk.) to stay under, remain, cheerful endurance

      iv. Biblically then, character is developed by undergoing sufferings – things in life that crowd, pressure or rub you the wrong way. But it is not about just going through sufferings but also cheerfully enduring them. This ability then will develop character, that quality that has been tested and refined so that what is left is valuable and precious, your character.

   b. The English definition of character is the combination of emotional, intellectual and moral qualities distinguishing one from another.

   c. Pastor Bill Hybels is known for his short statement, "Character is who you are when no one is looking."

   d. In Pastor Frank Damazio's book, *The Making Of A Leader*, character is defined in the following ways:

      i. Character is the seat of one's moral being.

      ii. Character is the inner life of man. It will reflect either the traits of the sinful nature (being influenced by the world) or the divine nature (being influenced by the Word of God).

      iii. Character is the combination of qualities distinguishing any person or class of persons.

6

     iv.   Character is the action of an individual when under pressure.

     v.   Finally, character is the sum total of all the negative and positive qualities in a person's life, exemplified by one's thoughts, values, motivations, attitudes, feelings, and actions.

2. **There are many Biblical examples of the development of character, both good and bad. In what ways can Joab's life negatively illustrate character flaws?**

  a. Joab was David's second-in-command, **1 Chr. 11:6; 27:34**, a mighty man in battle, nevertheless a man who had serious flaws in his character. God has always placed a greater premium on character than on one's abilities or gifts. History teaches that God will pass over someone with immense potential only to choose the one who seemingly doesn't have "the goods". Ability will invariably rank low on God's list of requirements for those who would be a leader because He wants you to learn what it means to trust in Him to get things done. Indeed, Jesus said that some have done great things without ever even knowing Him. **Matt. 7:21-23**

  b. Joab was **presumptuous** and presumption is always dangerous for leaders. James Lee Beall, in his book *Laying the Foundation,* says, "Presume comes from the Latin praesumere which means 'to anticipate, suppose, or take in advance.' The English definition is much closer to the Bible usage: it means 'to dare, to take too much upon one's self.' Those who presume take upon themselves authority that was not given to them. They overstep the limits of propriety and courtesy and intrude into places where they have no business. Contrary to what some may think, this is not aggressive faith, but blatant rebellion." **2 Sam. 3:22-27,** says about Joab's actions that "David did not know it." This was the ultimate in presumption.

  c. Joab was subtly **deceptive**. In **2 Sam. 14:1-8,** we see that through deception Joab subtly enticed David into doing something he would forever regret. Absalom deserved the death penalty for murder, and both Joab and David knew it. Joab's counsel came through a subtle side step around the righteous thing to do. A counselor is in a powerful position, which many a leader frequently finds himself filling. In trying to avoid having your ideas rejected it is all too easy to resort to the subtle deception of distorting facts or omitting things that would damage your presentation. Integrity demands that you clearly and concisely present your thoughts and then take a back seat, especially if you are not in the lead position.

   d. Joab was **self-serving**. In **2 Sam. 19:11-14, 22; 20:4-10,** Joab had definitely found a way to deal with his successor, he killed him. As the story proceeds we find that Joab's brother Abishai subordinates himself to Joab and allows Joab to once again take the place as commander of the army, **2 Sam. 20:22b-23.** Why didn't David take any action? The passage doesn't say, but we can probably safely say that David decided that this was the path of least resistance and greatest good for his kingdom. Yet God was not pleased. Look at what David said a few years later as he reveals his desire for justice in Joab's life in **1 Ki. 2:5-6.** *"Now you yourself know what Joab son of Zeruiah did to me — what he did to the two commanders of Israel's armies, Abner son of Ner and Amasa son of Jether. He killed them, shedding their blood in peacetime as if in battle, and with that blood stained the belt around his waist and the sandals on his feet. 6 Deal with him according to your wisdom, but do not let his gray head go down to the grave in peace."*

3. **What is the relationship between character and personal integrity?**

   a. Personal integrity is vital for all leaders. Your word, or your promise, no matter how small the situation, should be as reliable and trustworthy as God's. If you are not in control of the situation, then don't make any promises. The Hebrew definition for the word integrity is; uprightness, straightness, evenness, from - to be right, be straight, level, just, lawful. This will constantly be an ongoing need, leaders of integrity. Paul made an effort to always maintain a clear conscience, or a personal standard of integrity. **Acts 24:16** - *So I strive always to keep my conscience clear before God and man.*

   b. Financial integrity is vital for all leaders. As leaders in the kingdom of God you have a mandate to do all you can to be person of integrity when it comes to finances. In **1 Chr. 29:14, 17,** we see that God tests the heart and is pleased with financial integrity. *14 "But who am I, and who are my people, that we should be able to give as generously as this? Everything comes from you, and we have given you only what comes from your hand. 17 I know, my God, that you test the heart and are pleased with integrity. All these things have I given willingly and with honest intent. And now I have seen with joy how willingly your people who are here have given to you.* There will always be a need for leaders of integrity that have stood the test. Leaders that are financially right, straight, level, and just.

c. Financial integrity has always been a problem. In AD 394, Saint Jerome was asked how to avoid the temptations of the day by a fellow bishop. In his reply he pointed out many practical countermeasures that one could employ to "keep the straight path of Christ and not be led astray into the haunts of vice." As Jerome starts to address finances we see that the advice he gave then can still be valuable today. He said, "We (the clergy) should never ask for gifts, and seldom accept them even when begged to do so. Somehow or other the very man who offers you a present holds you the cheaper for accepting it; if you refuse, it is strange how much more admiration for you he feels. When you have received money to be spent on the poor, to be cautious with it while crowds are hungry, or (what is most obvious villainy) to take any of it for yourself, is to surpass the cruelty of the worst robber. It is the glory of a bishop to provide means for the poor, but is a disgrace for any priest to think of wealth for himself."

d. Paul decided that as a Christian leader it was important for him to set an example of hard work. He insisted that they follow his example and, in **2 Thess. 3:7-13**, he said one should never tire of doing what is right. *7 For you yourselves know how you ought to follow our example. We were not idle when we were with you, 8 nor did we eat anyone's food without paying for it. On the contrary, we worked night and day, laboring and toiling so that we would not be a burden to any of you. 9 We did this, not because we do not have the right to such help, but in order to make ourselves a model for you to follow. 10 For even when we were with you, we gave you this rule: "If a man will not work, he shall not eat." 11 We hear that some among you are idle. They are not busy; they are busybodies. 12 Such people we command and urge in the Lord Jesus Christ to settle down and earn the bread they eat. 13 And as for you, brothers, never tire of doing what is right.* That word, right, in the Greek means to act uprightly and is the outworking of integrity.

e. Here is a personal code of ethics for financial integrity.

   i.   I will always set an example for others by faithfully paying my tithes and cheerfully giving offerings to the local church.

   ii. Whatever my economic status, I will strive to be a generous giver whenever the opportunity avails itself.

9

iii. I will consider my verbal commitments as binding as a written contract.

iv. If I can't pay a bill on time, I'll contact my creditor, no matter how well I know him, and inform him of when he can expect payment.

v. By my attitude and straightforward practices, I will work to become a valued customer to all with whom I deal.

vi. I will never demand a discount, reduced rate, or free service NOT available to my non-Christian neighbor.

> (From an article by Stephen Bly in the Leadership magazine.)

DEVELOPING CHARACTER IN TITUS

1. **What is leadership?**

Leadership is the act of bringing people from one place to another. To lead is to influence people to choose, think, or act a certain way. To be a good leader you must have a destination in mind. Maybe you haven't been there yet, but you must be headed there, and you must be out in front of your followers.

2. **Who is a leader?**

a. Anyone can be a leader, and everyone can be a leader in some way.

b. Within the kingdom, though, there are certain individuals who have received the gift of leadership as mentioned in **Rom. 12:8.** *If it is encouraging, let him encourage; if it is contributing to the needs of others, let him give generously;* ***if it is leadership, let him govern diligently;*** *if it is showing mercy, let him do it cheerfully.* These gifted individuals are then called by God to lead.

c. Yet many of the traits of a gifted leader can also be taught and learned. Based on the old concept of nature versus nurture we see that while certain individuals are gifted (born as) leaders, everyone can be taught skills that enhance (develop) their ability to lead.

3. **Is it bad to want to be a leader?**

a. It is bad to want to be a leader when the desire is only motivated by self-centeredness.

b. *Should you then seek great things for yourself? Seek them not.* **Jer. 45:5**

c. When our desire to lead is motivated by a desire to serve other people in humility, and when we realize that being in a position of leadership is a privilege, not a right, then it is a godly desire.

d. *If anyone sets his heart on being an overseer, he desires a noble task.* **1 Tim 3:1**

e. In the New Testament the book of Titus gives one great insight into the realm of leadership development.

WHAT IS THE MESSAGE IN TITUS?

Titus 1:1-4

1 Paul, a servant of God and an apostle of Jesus Christ for the faith of God's elect and the knowledge of the truth that leads to godliness— 2 a faith and knowledge resting on the hope of eternal life, which God, who does not lie, promised before the beginning of time, 3 and at his appointed season he brought his word to light through the preaching entrusted to me by the command of God our Savior, 4 To Titus, my true son in our common faith: Grace, and peace from God the Father and Christ Jesus our Savior.

1. **Where does Christian leadership start?**

   Christian leadership starts with the message of the Gospel. Before Paul could address Titus' situation, he had to remind him of the big picture of salvation, the process of growth and of God's dealings in a leader's life. Before we can understand where God wants to take us, we need to understand what He has already done in us and for us.

2. **What two things do God's elect have?**

   a. God's elect have faith.

   *"For the **faith** of God's elect…"*

   Romans 12:3 – Faith comes as a gift from God.

   Romans 10:17 – Faith comes by hearing the Word of God.

   Ephesians 2:8-10 – We are saved through faith.

   God is the source of our faith. When we have faith, it is never that we are doing God a favor, it is HIM doing US a favor. **Romans 5:17** … *how much more will those who* ***receive*** *God's abundant provision of grace and of the gift of righteousness reign in life through the one man, Jesus Christ.* The word *"receive"* in the Greek means *"to take."* When God offers us something, we still need to lay hold of it and take it from Him.

b. God's elect have knowledge

"*...and the **knowledge** of the truth...*"

The Greek word used here is *epignosis*. It implies full discernment and revelation. It comes from the root word *gnosis*, which means "to come to know, in a personal abstract way." But *epignosis* is a stronger word; not just coming to know, but knowing fully. This full knowledge is God's desire for both His people and His leaders.

1 Corinthians 13:12 – *Then I shall know fully, even as I am fully known.*

Colossians 1:9-10 – *Fill you with knowledge ... Grow in knowledge.*

3. **What is the purpose of faith and knowledge?**

Faith and knowledge should affect your lifestyle. "*...That leads to Godliness.*" **James 1:22-25** *22 Do not merely listen to the word, and so deceive yourselves. Do what it says. 23 Anyone who listens to the word but does not do what it says is like a man who looks at his face in a mirror 24 and, after looking at himself, goes away and immediately forgets what he looks like. 25 But the man who looks intently into the perfect law that gives freedom, and continues to do this, not forgetting what he has heard, but doing it — he will be blessed in what he does.*

God's grace both gives us faith, and simultaneously changes us to do good works. A theme of Titus is that we are not saved by good works, but we are saved to do good works.

4. **What do faith and knowledge rest on?**

Faith and Knowledge rest on hope. Hope can be defined as "*anticipation (with pleasure), expectation, or confidence.*" Or just, "*pleasurable anticipation.*" The difference between a baby Christian and a mature Christian is hope. True hope must be developed. In view of the coming statements on the character of a leader or elder, Paul is here laying a foundation for the basics in a leader's life.

5. **When was this all set in order?**

a. This was all set in order by God before the beginning of time. **Titus 1:2,** "*...Which God, who does not lie, set in* *order before the beginning of time."* The Greek word used for time is chronos, which means a span or length of time. God's plan was started before time ever began to be measured. Look **up 2 Timothy 1:9-10** and **Ephesians 1:4, 5, 11** to understand how God's eternal plan for us was revealed. In context of what he is about to say about leaders, Paul is setting up the concept that God has chosen leaders from before time began to further His plans for the world and His kingdom. Jeremiah was told much the same thing in **Jer. 1:4** – *Before I formed you in the womb I knew you, before you were born I set you apart; I appointed you as a prophet to the nation.*

b. Since God had everything planned from before the beginning of time, we can take comfort knowing that right now, He knew from eternity past where you would be and what you would be going through. He has a plan!

6. When did this all take place?

a. This was all revealed in God's appointed season. **Titus 1:3** "*...And at His appointed season he brought his word to light...*" The Greek word for *season* is *kairos* which means a set or specified time, set apart by a certain marked event. God has a specific purpose for events.

b. **1 Peter 5:5-6** – Waiting for God's "due time" is a process all leaders must go through.

c. **Hebrews 6:10-12** – Waiting for God's "due time" involves both faith and patience.

d. **Hebrews 6:13-15** – Waiting for God's "due time" was how Abraham was able to receive his promise.

e. Abraham waited for Isaac for 25 years, Jacob waited to receive his inheritance for 20 years, Joseph had to wait 13 years for his dreams even to begin being fulfilled, and David waited 13 years to be a king and 20 years to be king over all Israel.

7. What does this mean for us?

God often gives us glimpses of His will long before he brings those things to pass, just like He did with Abraham, Jacob, Joseph, David, and many others. But we cannot despise the days of small beginnings (**Zech. 4:10**). The things that God promises He will always bring to pass (**2 Cor. 1:20**). Think about this, when someone makes a promise, it is their responsibility to follow through and keep the promise. It is not up to the person who received the promise to make anything happen. When God promises us something, it is up to Him to keep His word. We do not need to worry about forcing Him to do anything for us. We can trust Him.

WHAT WAS TITUS' MISSION?

The reason I left you in Crete was that you might put in order what was left unfinished and appoint elders in every town, as I directed you. **Titus 1:5**

1. **What was Titus' mission?**

   Titus' Mission was to fix the problems in the church and appoint elders. In other words, he was to take people out of an ungodly culture and transform them into leaders/elders in God's kingdom.

2. **What authority did Titus have to do this work?**

   Just as nations are ruled by governments, so God has a government in place to oversee his church. As an apostle, Paul had authority over the universal church, and he gave Titus a similar authority over the churches in Crete, to appoint local church leaders. He gave the same charge to Timothy in **2 Timothy 2:2** *And the things you have heard me say in the presence of many witnesses entrust to reliable men who will also be qualified to teach others.*

3. **What structure does this government have?**

   a. The structure of God's government is laid out in **Ephesians 4:11-12,** where Paul lists five ascension gift ministries (or fivefold-ministries, as they are sometimes called).

      i. *Apostles* – The word means "Sent one" The term was originally used for Greek and Roman generals in charge of changing the culture of a battle or a conquered city. In the early church, apostles were father figures with great authority, sent by God to affect the people and change their culture.

      ii. *Prophets* – Men and Women who were separated to God in order to hear Him speaking and then to speak to the people, challenging them on His behalf.

      iii. *Evangelists* – People sent to equip God's people to share the good news.

      iv. *Pastors/Teachers* – Sent to strengthen the body of Christ by teaching the word and caring for the flock.

   b. The function of these gifted people is to do for the church what Christ Himself did for His disciples, equip them to do the work of ministry. In other words the ascension gift ministries were given to the church to equip every person to do the ministry to which God has called them.

4. Who was the prophet Paul spoke about?

One of Crete's own prophets has said it: 'Cretans are always liars, evil brutes, lazy gluttons.' This saying is true. Therefore rebuke them sharply, so that they will be sound in the faith." **Titus 1:12-13**

Epimenides was a famous Greek philosopher who had lived 700 years previously. According to legend, he wandered into a magical forest where he fell asleep for seventy years. When he awoke he found that he possessed all knowledge.

5. Why did Paul quote Epimenides?

He used a quote from within classical Greek literature to illustrate the character of the people with whom Titus had to work. Paul's quote was also to show that the people of Crete were set in their sinful and cultural ways. They had been this way for over 700 years.

6. So what culture was prevalent on Crete?

a. *Liars* – From the Greek *cretizo*, the word was slang for *liar*, but was originally derived from their nationality. In essence, it was a racial slur.

b. *Evil Brutes* – This implies that their character was savage and animal-like.

c. *Lazy Gluttons* – This refers to their uncontrolled greed in every aspect of life.

d. That is what Titus had to work with… so what do you have to work with? What is your culture's dominate sins?

WHAT IS AN ELDER/LEADER?

Titus 1:6-9

6 An elder must be blameless, the husband of but one wife, a man whose children believe and are not open to the charge of being wild and disobedient. 7 Since an overseer is entrusted with God's work, he must be blameless — not overbearing, not quick-tempered, not given to drunkenness, not violent, not pursuing dishonest gain. 8 Rather he must be hospitable, one who loves what is good, who is self-controlled, upright, holy and disciplined. 9 He must hold

15

firmly to the trustworthy message as it has been taught, so that he can encourage others by sound doctrine and refute those who oppose it.

1. **God is looking for what kind of person?**

   This passage (along with **1 Timothy 3:1-8**), provides a list of qualifications that a person must meet in order to be considered for a leadership position within the church.

2. **What are the qualifications for a leader?**

   They must... The first set of qualifications deal with a leader's home life. You need to be a leader in private before you can become one in public. The home is the training ground for all Godly leaders.

   a. *Be blameless* – A leader must hold themselves to the highest moral standards. And within the context of the verse it seems that this blameless life must first be exhibited within his family.

   b. *Be the husband of one wife* – No polygamy. The phrase literally means "a one-woman man." This is not addressing the issue of divorce, but rather multiple wives.

   c. *Have believing children* – Cross reference with **1 Timothy 3:4**, which merely says children must be "submissive." A leader must first be a good parent, as evidenced in the life of their children. This does not mean that all of a leader's/elder's children must be saved. That would override the free will nature of salvation. However if none of a leader's children are saved then it would reflect on their lack of parenting skills in bringing up a child in the training and instruction of the Lord. **(Eph. 6:4)**

   They must not... A set of disqualifications. These issues should be warning signs that a person is not quite ready for the responsibility of leadership, or possibly not even called to such a position. These qualities must not be looked on as absolutes, but rather set standards that every leader should be striving to attain.

   a. *Be overbearing* – Arrogant, self-willed, or self-pleasing.

   b. *Be quick-tempered* – Hot-headed, quick to start an argument.

   c. *Be given to drunkenness* – See **Ephesians 5:18**, drunkenness is sin.

d. *Be violent* – Violence and anger is a deep-rooted problem.

e. *Be pursuing dishonest gain* – Wendell Smith's book *Great Faith* states:

    i. Pursuing prosperity is godly! **Gen. 12:2; Mal. 3:10; 2 Cor. 9:6-11**

    ii. Pursuing dishonest gain is wicked. Flee from it - **1 Timothy 6:6-11**

    iii. Prosperity must have a purpose. Extending the kingdom of God is our purpose.

        • Egypt was the land of <u>not</u> enough.

        • The Wilderness was the land of <u>just</u> enough

        • Canaan was the land of <u>more</u> than enough.

They must...   Another set of qualifying characteristics a leader must possess. Paul here begins to develop the theme that although salvation does not come because of our own goodness, yet because we are saved we are enabled to be people of great virtue.

a. *Be hospitable* – Implies a devotion to the welfare of others. **Rom. 12:13**.

b. *Be a lover of good* – Good things or good people. **Mt 22:36-40** - For Christians, loving God and people is the same thing.

c. *Be self-controlled* – Sound in mind, literally "moderate as to opinion or passion."

d. *Be upright* – See holy – the two statements in the Greek are tied together.

e. *Be holy* – **1 Peter 1:15-16** - Holy = physically pure, morally blameless, and spiritually consecrated.

f. *Be disciplined* – This word means to plan on delaying or denying gratification.

g. *Hold firmly to sound doctrine* – **Ephesians 4:14.** Don't be blown around by shifting opinions. Stick to the solid doctrines of the word of God.

3. What was wrong with the Cretan's culture?

The issues that confronted Titus in discipling Cretans are found in every culture and must be confronted by every Christian leader.

Titus 1:10-12 - *For there are many rebellious people, mere talkers and deceivers, especially those of the circumcision* *group. They must be silenced, because they are ruining whole households by teaching things they ought not to teach — and that for the sake of dishonest gain.*

a. *Rebellion* - deals with authority

The word means "insubordinate in fact or temper." You have authority when you are under authority. Satan doesn't want anyone to have authority so he will try to get everyone to rebel. See also **2 Peter 2:10, Numbers 16:3, Isaiah 14:12, Revelation 12:1-9**

b. *Mere talkers* - deals with speech

Refers to idle, senseless or mischievous talk; our words are more powerful than we know. God used words to create, and we are made in His image. See **Proverbs 18:21, Ephesians 5:4, and 1 John 3:18**

c. *Deceivers* - deals with truth

Some people intentionally mislead the mind. This is deadly. What a person believes to be true will determine everything about them, even the course of their life. If a person is deceived it will completely pervert everything they believe. **Revelation 12:9** and **James 1:22**. Jesus is *the truth.*

d. *Dishonest gain* - deals with the dishonest use of money

WHAT METHOD WAS TITUS TO USE?
Titus 2:1 - 3:15

1. What was Paul's answer to Cretan culture?

Paul exhorted five separate groups of people, (older men, younger men, older women, younger women, and slaves) to conduct themselves in a similar fashion. It is a different lifestyle that sets believers apart from the world. There are three qualities that he expected each of these groups to exhibit.

a. *Self-Controlled* – The word means "Sound in mind, moderate as to opinion or passion." **Galatians 5:22-23** says being self-controlled is a fruit of the Spirit.
- **1:5-8** – to elders

    - **2:1-2** – to older men

    - **2:3-5** – to older and then younger women

    - **2:6** – to young men
b. *Disciplined* – "Strong in a thing, masterful, self-controlled in appetite." One who denies or delays gratification.

- **1:8** – to elders – they must be disciplined

c. *Temperate* – "To keep sober or to abstain from wine."

- **2:2** – the older men, already described as lazy gluttons who needed temperance

- **1 Tim. 3:2** – bishops or overseers were to be temperate

- **1 Tim. 3:11** – the deaconess or the women were to be temperate

2. **How do we confront culture today?**

Today we confront culture the same way that Paul did, and the same way that he urged Titus and Timothy to use.

a. **Through teaching the Word of God.**

-**Titus 2:1-4, 7, 9, 12, 15 1 Timothy 4:11-13, 2 Timothy 4:2, and 1 Peter 4:11** all refer to teaching or preaching the Word.

-The church is the most influential body on earth because whenever it comes together, every arena of society is represented, and they are all there to listen to one person, the preacher/teacher. Culture can be confronted and transformed through the teaching of the Word. Teaching the Word will bring revelation of the standards for character that God has already established for every culture in the world. God's standards transcends the authority of every culture. When the culture does not line up with the Word, then that culture must be challenged and bow to the Word.

b. **Through example and life-style.**

-**Titus 2:7, 1 Corinthians 11:1** - Follow me as I follow Christ.

-Words and actions are equal in importance. If you don't practice what you preach you are a hypocrite and will have no authority. The importance of living a Godly life and being an example cannot be over emphasized. The next generation of leaders must have a model, examples, of leaders who have attained to God's standards.

c. **Through encouragement or rebuke.**

-**Titus 1:9, 13; 2:6, 15; 2 Timothy 4:2**

-This must be done with great patience. It can take a long time for people's habits to change. Don't give up if you don't see fruit blossom overnight. However, God is still capable of transforming lives in an instant. Don't count out the possibility of transformational miracles. *Encouragement* would be the positive side of this coin and *Rebuke* the negative. Both are needed in developing the next generation of leaders.

DESCRIBING CHARACTER IN 1 TIMOTHY

1 Tim. 6:11-12 - *But you, man of God, flee from all this, and pursue righteousness, godliness, faith, love, endurance and gentleness. Fight the good fight of the faith. Take hold of the eternal life to which you were called when you made your good confession in the presence of many witnesses.*
Here Paul was addressing his son in the faith who was the leader at the church of Ephesus.

1. **What should be the character of this man of God?**

    a. *Flee from all this...*

    Flee from an inappropriate love of;

    i.   Money – **1 Tim. 6:3-10** – not money itself, but the desire to get rich

    ii.   Idols – **1 Cor. 10:14** – an idol is anything that you worship besides God

    iii.   Sex – **1 Cor. 6:18** – *porneia* – any sex outside of marriage

2. *Follow after or Pursue...*

    Paul's metaphor suggest that these qualities are running away from you and you must run after them, or pursue them, in order to have them be a part of your life. In other words, these qualities are not normally part of a person's life but must be aggressively sought after on a regular basis.

    a. *Righteousness* – towards people – that state of him who is such as he ought to be

    b. *Godliness* – towards God – to be devout in all your ways

    c. *Faith* – firm persuasion, conviction of the truth of anything

    d. *Love* – a divine, sacrificial love towards others, a giving of one's self

    e. *Endurance* – patience – cheerfully enduring any trial or suffering

    f. *Gentleness* – mild, meek, humble

3. **Fight the good fight of the faith...**

a. The good fight – can be against both your old nature and your old enemy

      i. **Col. 3:5-10** – fight your old nature through taking off, putting on and renewing

      ii. **James 4:7** – resist the devil and he will flee from you

b. Take hold of eternal life – All allusions are to the Greek games – fight, conquer and seize the prize; carry off the crown of eternal life!

Conclusion:

This was the charge to both Titus and Timothy, and this is still the charge to any leader in the church. In every village and every major city the leader's task is to reach into the culture of their location, preach the gospel and then train those who respond. The qualifications are clear. The challenge is great. But the good news is that we are co-workers with Jesus, part of His gifts to the church to see that the next generation of leaders are equipped to do what God has called them to do – extend His kingdom around the world!

And the things you have heard me say in the presence of many witnesses entrust to reliable people who will be qualified to teach others. **2 Tim. 2:2**

Section 2

CONDUCT
How you live…

CONDUCT – HOW YOU LIVE

In discussing the preparation of a leader and how they should conduct themselves in ministry, one of the first items to be explored is that of the call of God. God has a call for everyone – but not all are called to a leadership role. In this section the focus will be mainly on those called to lead, but in reality all believers should have similar lifestyle requirements.

HOW CAN GOD'S CALL BE DISCERNED?

1. **Where does the call to lead come from?**

   a. **John 15:16** - You did not choose me... Every call must come out of being with Him, not personal ambition, or for a position in the community, or a desire to sit around all day studying and praying, or a desire to travel and lecture from your lofty perch!

   b. **Acts 4:13** - They took note of them that they had been with Jesus! A self-sent minister is a stench to God and man! But if you have been in the presence of the Lord then others can't help but notice.

   c. **Luke 3:2-3** - The word of God came to John – so he went preaching. When God makes His call on your life evident then you must take action. This might not mean immediately quitting everything else you are doing, but you must be willing to make any changes God is asking of you.

   d. **John 20:21** - HE must send us – "so send I you". Self-sent people will invariably become shipwreck, lacking the call, the authority, the power and the vision to do what they are calling themselves to do.

   e. **Matt. 9:38** - Ask the Lord of the harvest, therefore, to send out workers into His harvest field. God says that the harvest is ready, which must mean that in every generation and in every place the Spirit of God is working and preparing people to receive the gospel message. What God wants is for us to focus on the laborers. Pray for the workers, the harvesters, the called ones.

   f. **Rom. 10:15** - How can they preach unless they are sent?

2. **What does a False Call look like?**

   a. All are called to spread the Gospel.

      Mark 16:15-17 - go into all the world

      Acts 1:8 - you will receive power

      Acts 11:19-22 - telling them the good news

b. Some are called to full time service - their whole lives involved.

c. Some presume to call themselves but invariably suffer for doing so.

    2 Sam. 18:19-31 - Ahimaaz - was not the one to go but he went anyway.

    To the Cushite – "Go, tell the King what you have seen" (21).

    Lev. 10:1-2 - Nadab & Abihu... died in their presumption!

    2 Chr. 26:16-21 – In his presumption Uzziah tried to offer incense but leprosy was his reward.

3. **What does the True Call look like?**

    a. **John 15:16** - I chose you... yet there is no set pattern in how God will call you to your ministry. In fact it seems that God has an infinite variety of ways in which He calls. Webster's Dictionary says the definition of the word "call" is, to summon to a specific duty, to command or ask to come. Someone asked Emily Post, "What is the correct procedure when one is invited to the White House of the United States and has a previous engagement?" She answered, "An invitation to lunch or dine at the White House is a command, and automatically cancels any other engagement!" When God communicates His call on your life then all other desires seem to pale in significance.

    b. **1 Kings 19:19** – As soon as the mantle touched Elisha, he knew he was called. His response was to immediately make preparations to answer that call.

    c. **Amos 7:14-15** – Amos responded to the call of God and realized that the Lord had taken him from the most humble of states. Don't let your current job, or lack thereof, affect you when you hear God's call.

    d. **1 Sam. 16:13** – David was called when the horn of oil was poured on him.

    e. **Acts 13:2** – Saul's call was confirmed through the ministry of a "Presbytery" – or when the "body of elders" sets someone into their place of calling through the laying on of hands with prophecy. This pattern was first established in the Old Testament, when it was time for Joshua to succeed Moses. In **Numbers 27:18-23** we see that this ceremony of confirmation had certain factors. It was before the leadership (Eleazar), in front of the people, and hands were laid on Joshua as he was commissioned. In **Acts 13:1-3**, much the same ceremony took place over Saul and Barnabus with certain key factors added. Prayer, worship, fasting and prophecy were incorporated. This process became an ongoing pattern for it subsequently happened over Timothy's life. **1 Tim. 1:18** speaks of the prophecies that went over Timothy's life. **1 Tim. 4:14** admonished Timothy to not neglect the gift (charisma) that was given him when the body of elders (Presbytery) laid their hands on him. How did Paul know all this**? 2 Tim. 1:6** reminds Timothy to stir up the gift (charisma) of God that was given him when Paul had personally laid his hands on him. Obviously Paul was part of that body of elders and remembered full well what gifts and callings were confirmed and imparted to Timothy at that time.

4. **Whom will He call to lead?**

   a. **Heb. 11:6** - He rewards those who earnestly seek Him

   b. **Acts 10:34** - God does not show favoritism, yet some qualifications seem to be standard.

      i. A voice that is understandable

      ii. An appearance that is not objectionable

      iii. An average amount of brain power

5. **How is one called to lead?**

   a. Invariably one is called through the dealings of God as God breathes on our lives and we yearn to serve Him.

   b. Our desire is overshadowed by our feelings of unworthiness.

      i. **Moses - Ex. 3:1-6; 4:1, 10, 13** – Five times Moses responds negatively to God's call on his life.

         • Inadequacy in 3:11 – who am I?

         • Ignorance in 3:13 – who are you?

         • Incredibility in 4:1 – who will listen?

         • Inarticulateness in 4:11 – but I can't speak!

         • Insubordination in 4:13 – send someone else!

      ii. **Gideon - Judges 6:11-13, 15, 17; 6:36-40** – Here is an intellectual man with clearly thought out questions for Jehovah.

         • His first response to the angel was why – why then has all this happened to us?

         • His follow up question was where are all the miracles that our fathers told us about?

- Then begins the dialogue that results in several miraculous signs given to Gideon.

iii. **Isaiah - Isa. 6:1-9** - Here am I, SEND ME!

- No real questions.

- Immediate repentance.

- Immediate acquiescence to the will of God – here am I, send me. This is truly the pattern response that God would have from every called one.

- Our feelings should lead us to trust in His sufficiency.

  1) **2 Cor. 3:5** - our sufficiency is of God

  2) **Phil. 2:13** - For it is God who works in you...

  3) **Phil. 4:13** - I can - through Him

  4) **1 Cor. 9:16-17** - Woe is me if I preach not the gospel!

The preparation of a leader begins with responding to God's call on one's life. But then the real work begins. While character is being developed one's conduct must change. God has set His standards high and challenges every potential leader to start focusing on making changes so that their outward conduct is something that can be exemplified. Let's look now at how God prepares leaders.

HOW CAN GODLY CONDUCT BE DEVELOPED?

2 Tim. 2:15 – *Do your best to present yourself to God as one approved, a workman who does not need to be ashamed and who correctly handles the word of truth.*

1 Tim. 3:1-13

1 Here is a trustworthy saying: If anyone sets his heart on being an overseer, he desires a noble task. 2 Now the overseer must be above reproach, the husband of but one wife, temperate, self-controlled, respectable, hospitable, able to teach, 3 not given to drunkenness, not violent but gentle, not quarrelsome, not a lover of money. 4 He must manage his own family well and see that his children obey him with proper respect. 5(If anyone does not know how to manage his own family, how can he take care of God's church?) 6 He must not be a recent convert, or he may become conceited and fall under the same judgment as the devil. 7 He must also have a good reputation with outsiders, so that he will not fall into disgrace and into the devil's trap.

8 Deacons, likewise, are to be men worthy of respect, sincere, not indulging in much wine, and not pursuing dishonest gain. 9 They must keep hold of the deep truths of the faith with a clear conscience. 10 They must first be tested; and then if there is nothing against them, let them serve as deacons. 11 In the same way, their wives are to be women worthy of respect, not malicious talkers but temperate and trustworthy in everything. 12 A deacon must be the husband of but one wife and must manage his children and his household well. 13 Those who have served well gain an excellent standing and great assurance in their faith in Christ Jesus.

1. **A leader must have experienced the basics of *salvation*.**

   a. **Acts 2:38-39** – Every leader should have experienced all parts of Peter's package; repentance, water baptism and the baptism of the Holy Spirit.

      i. Simply having the Holy Spirit is not divine approval of your perfection, but you must have the Holy Spirit to produce holiness in your life.

      ii. **Acts 3:12** - It was not Peter's holiness that healed.

      iii. **Acts 14:11-18** – The apostles stopped the people from sacrificing to them for knew who and what they were, and were not!

   b. **Ps. 50:16-17** - *But to the wicked, God says: "What right have you to recite my laws or take my covenant on your lips? You hate my instruction and cast my words behind you.*

   c. **1 Cor. 2:14-16** - The things of the Spirit are spiritually discerned and without conversion then the Word is a mystery to one and all.

   d. **Micah 3:8** - But as for me, I am filled with power, with the Spirit of the Lord...

   e. **Zech. 4:6** - Not by man's might or power, but by the Spirit of the Lord.

2. **A leader must first learn and then *share*.**

   a. Heb. 5:12-14 - who by constant use have trained themselves to distinguish good from evil.

   b. "The Christian teacher himself must first learn the things which he is to teach. It will be his prerogative not only to teach doctrine and the general outline of Christian faith but also the actual experiences through which Christians pass in every-day life. The enemy certainly is not theoretical; he is real and intensely active. He brings against each Christian every conceivable line of attack. It is the Pastor's business to take his people by the hand and lead them through bewildering and confusing experiences. While the enemy seeks to defeat and down them, it is the Pastor's job to lift them up and establish them in the faith. He is quite unqualified for such ministry unless he himself has gone through similar experiences. One has to go through the mill himself in order to be made bread for others. The discovery of Christ as the "form of the Fourth" who is with us in our burning fiery furnace will give us positiveness and joy as we explain to others who are passing through their fiery trial that ever near them too there will be found the presence of the Son of God." [John Riggs]

3. **A leader must come to a place of complete *surrender*.**

   a. No one is in a position to serve God effectively who with-holds ought from Him.

   b. We may serve him fairly well for a while with un-surrendered areas still in our lives, but the time will come that God will move to strip us of anything that stands between Him and us.

   c. **Gen. 35:1-3** – Later in his life Jacob finally rids himself of foreign gods although God had met him several times already.

      i. **Gen. 28:10-22** - Bethel experience

      ii. **Gen. 31:3** - Called to return

      iii. **Gen. 32:22-32** - Peniel - name changed

   d. God is a jealous God wanting 100% of our love and devotion.

      i. **Matt. 10:37** – No one person can be loved more than Jesus!

      ii. **Lk. 14:26, 27, 33** – We must be willing to give up all we have to follow.

   e. **Jn. 6:66** - Many disciples reach certain points and quit following Him.

   f. When you fall by the wayside you disqualify yourself from immediate service, restoration is possible, but always at great cost!

   g. **1 Cor. 9:24-27** - Let's not disqualify ourselves!

      i. **John Mark** – is a case history of disqualification **and** restoration.

      ii. **1 Pet. 5:13** - Peter called him his son in the Lord.

      iii. **Acts 12:12** – Written in early 44 AD the first mention of John shows his Jewish heritage.

iv. **Acts 12:25** – he went from Jerusalem to Antioch

v. **Acts 13:2-5** – John was their helper, minister = under oarsmen, servant, assistant

vi. **Acts 13:13** – Written in late 44 AD, John went home, but why? Perhaps he didn't like the servant's role? Maybe he was discouraged? Lazy? Lonely? Homesick?

vii. **Acts 15:37-38** – Written in 50 AD - 5 years later Paul still has a problem with John Mark's defection and says "he had deserted them."

Although we have no record of John's rehabilitation, or restoration, he surely must have worked the principles and applied himself for Barnabas to feel that he was again worthy to be used in his ministry. It probably took Paul a longer time to receive his ministry.

viii. **Col. 4:10** – Written in early 62 AD or 18 years after his defection Paul says, "receive him now."

ix. **2 Tim. 4:11** – Written in 66 or 67 AD - 22 years later John is now "helpful".

God is a God of grace and restoration... But, how much better if the young man would have applied himself and had always been helpful, or profitable in ministry.

4. **A leader is frequently called to *sacrifice*.**

a. **Rom. 12:1** - present your bodies a living sacrifice

b. **2 Cor. 1:4-11** - we felt the sentence of death

c. **Eph. 5:2** - as an offering and a sacrifice to God

d. **Phil. 2:17-18** - NIV - poured out like a drink offering

e. **Gen. 22:1-18** - Abraham was called upon to sacrifice his own and dearest, the one in whom were involved the promises of God. It was by his response to this call and his unhesitating willingness to give God his all that moved God to call him "His friend".

f. Baker - "Others may, I may not."

g. Champions make their own rules... and they are always tough!

h. **2 Sam. 24:24** - I will not sacrifice...offerings that cost me nothing!

5. **Every leader will experience times of *spiritual waiting*.**

a. When God would make a Moses, and have him prepared for spiritual and administrative leadership of His nation Israel, He not only chose a man who was the most highly trained of all the men of Egypt, but he took particular care that his servant had a long period of spiritual waiting! In the desert Moses shrank, but God grew. **Heb. 11:24-27**

b. David - anointed by Samuel, yet running for his life.

c. Paul - living in Tarsus for up to 5 years before Barnabus brought him back into ministry in Antioch.

d. There is something that one cannot learn in books, on battlefields or athletic fields, in laboratories, libraries, or lecture halls. There is a **fire** that God alone must kindle!

HOW IS A SERVANT MENTALITY DEVELOPED IN LEADERS?

1. **By following Jesus' example. Mark 10:35-45**

35 Then James and John, the sons of Zebedee, came to him. "Teacher," they said, "we want you to do for us whatever we ask." 36 "What do you want me to do for you?" he asked. 37 They replied, "Let one of us sit at your right and the other at your left in your glory." 38 "You don't know what you are asking," Jesus said. "Can you drink the cup I drink or be baptized with the baptism I am baptized with?" 39 "We can," they answered. Jesus said to them, "You will drink the cup I drink and be baptized with the baptism I am baptized with, 40 but to sit at my right or left is not for me to grant. These places belong to those for whom they have been prepared." 41 When the ten heard about this, they became indignant with James and John. 42 Jesus called them together and said, "You know that those who are regarded as rulers of the Gentiles lord it over them, and their high officials exercise authority over them. 43 Not so with you. Instead, whoever wants to become great among you must be your servant, 44 and whoever wants to be first must be slave of all. 45 For even the Son of Man did not come to be served, but to serve, and to give his life as a ransom for many."

a. (vss. 35-39) Leaders must guard themselves against having a self-reliant attitude that "I can" fulfill God's will for my life all on my own.

b. A desire for greatness is not, in itself, sinful. It is the motivation that determines its character.

   2 Kings 2:1-14 – Elisha asked for and received a double portion

c. (vss. 41-45) The disciple's attitude showed *selfish ambition*, but Jesus wanted them to seek to serve, not to seek personal benefits or pleasures.

   Jer. 45:1-5 – To Baruch – Seek them not!

2. By following Paul's examples. Phil. 2:1-30

    a. (vss. 3-4) A leader's motivation must be a Godly desire to help others rather than *selfish ambition.*

    b. (vss. 5-7) Successful leaders are successful *servants.* Those called to be leaders are not called to be different and above other people.

    c. (vss. 12,13 & 16,17) Although service to others may be 'draining', a leader's *success* is determined by the progress of those he serves.

    In *My Utmost for His Highest,* Oswald Chambers wrote the following.

    "According to Jesus Christ, he (a leader) is called to be a 'doormat' for others – called to be their spiritual leader, but never their superior. Paul said, "I know how to be abased…" (Phil. 4:12). Paul's idea of service was to pour his life out to the last drop for others. But the chief motivation behind Paul's service was not love for others but love for his Lord. If our devotion is to the cause of humanity, we will be quickly defeated and broken-hearted, since we will often be confronted with a great deal of ingratitude from other people. But if we are motivated by our love for God, no amount of ingratitude will be able to hinder us from serving one another."

    d. (vss. 19-21) A leader must take genuine *interest* in the lives of those they serve.

    e. (vss. 29-30) A true servant is willing to *risk their life* to accomplish their mission.

WHAT ARE SOME OF THE PERSONAL TRAITS OF A LEADER?

1. A gift of leadership is the ability to motivate and lead others in accomplishing God's purposes. Rom. 12:8

    a. God will equip you for whatever He calls you to do.

    b. In God's will is God's provision.

        i.   **Heb. 13:20-21** – God will equip us with whatever we need to do His will.

        ii.   **1 Thess. 5:24** – The one who calls you is faithful, and he will do it.

2. In order to be effective a leader must develop spiritual maturity.

    a. **2 Chron. 1:7-12** – Solomon's request

    b. **Rom. 5:3-4** – God's Process for Maturity

c. A leader's maturity is revealed when he deals with people.

    i. **2 Kings 14:1-21** – David listened to Joab and the actress of Tekoa

    ii. **2 Sam. 12:1-13** – David repented at and Nathan's rebuke

    iii. **2 Sam. 16:1-14** – David ignored Shimei's cursing

d. Examples of immaturity in a leader can be seen in the following.

    i. **2 Chron. 10:1-13** – Rehoboam rejected counsel and the people

    ii. **Luke 9:52-54** – The Sons of Thunder wanted to execute the people

e. Personal immaturity can be seen in the following traits.

    i. Little tact in getting along with people. **Pro. 10:32; 12:18**

    ii. Interfering in the affairs of others. **2 Thess. 3:11**

    iii. Resisting change. **Pro. 15:31-32**

    iv. Blaming others when things go wrong. **Gen. 3:12**

    v. Inability to handle criticism. **Pro. 10:17**

HOW DO LEADERS DEVELOP COMMUNICATION SKILLS?

1. **Communication Defined**

a. Webster's Dictionary gives the following; to impart to another or others; to bestow or confer for joint possession; to share, to participate.

b. Within the Church it can be defined as, the interaction necessary for individuals to relate together in a group effort aimed at accomplishing its ministry goals.

2. **Two Basic Ways to Frustrate Communication**

a. When a person does not feel like you respect their feelings.

b. When people do not sense that you are really listening to them.

3. **Basic Principles for Successful Communication**

a. Work at listening.   **Pro. 18:13**   **James 1:19**

b. Ask questions. Don't assume, clarify.

c. Avoid distractions. Focus on the speaker, don't watch others or let your mind wander.

d. Be patient. It is far better to spend a few extra minutes at the beginning when you are communicating to others a new idea, than to spend a lot of time undoing what they have done because they didn't understand exactly what to do.

e. Avoid anger and arguments.

2 Tim. 2:24, 25   James 1:20   Pro. 6:16-19

4. **The Importance of Good Communication**

a. It promotes a sense of being a part of the team.

b. It will clearly convey the group's goals.

c. It makes change efficient

d. It keeps misinformation and gossip at a minimum.

Pro. 27:17 – As iron sharpens iron, so one man sharpens another.

HOW IMPORTANT IS MOTIVATION TO A LEADER?

1. **We are in a battle**

Satan is continually working against the purposes of God and trying to undermine your progress through discouragement, oppression and other obstacles.

Heb. 12:12 – Strengthen the feeble arms and weak knees.

2. **We must fight spiritual laziness**

The carnal nature must be disciplined to prevent spiritual laziness.

Matt. 26:41 – The spirit is willing but the body is weak.

3. **We must recognize these factors that motivate Christians to serve**

a. Relationship to Jesus - **Luke 7:36-47; 1 Cor. 15:9-10**

b. A person's sense of calling - **Rom. 1:1**

c. The visionary level of the Pastor – **Pro. 29:18**

d. The example of others – **2 Thess. 3:7**

e. Exhortation - **2 Tim. 1:6**

4. **We must keep lighting the fire**

a. Create a dynamic vision – this is where I want to go and why.

b. Set your goals, involving others in the process – how can we get there?

c. Build confidence – be positive.

d. Over communicate.

e. Practice absolute honesty.

f. Take full responsibility.

g. Focus on serving and support – not control.

h. When the time is right, take a leap of faith.

i. Follow up, and expect to make adjustments.

j. Never, never, never give up!

HOW CAN EXCELLENCE BE DEVELOPED?

1. By following David's and Solomon's examples

a. **2 Sam. 7:1-4** – after 440 years of established worship to Jehovah, David had a new idea… "I want to build a temple for the presence of the Lord."

b. **1 Chr. 28:1a** – some 30 years later David summons all his leaders.

c. **1 Chr. 28:2-6** – David shares his vision.

d. **I Chr. 28:11a** – He gives to Solomon 30 years' worth of instructions.

e. **I Kings 6:1** – It took Solomon 4 more years to get ready to build.

f. **I Kings 6:38b** – It took Solomon 7 years to build this Temple, the most glorious structure ever built by the Jews – a project of **excellence**!

2. By making excellence your goal

a. **Eccl. 9:10**

b. **Col. 3:23-24**

c. If it's worth doing… it's worth doing with **excellence**.

3. By understanding the difference between excellence and perfection

a. Striving for perfection leads to condemnation.

b. Striving for excellence produces a superior effort without condemnation.

c. Strive for excellence in your primary area of calling and ministry. Yet, always continue to pursue growth in your weak areas. Guard your priorities.

4. By recognizing that personal excellence requires

continual growth in 3 areas

a. Personality – Whether melancholic or sanguine, strive for growth.

b. Gifts – Drawing closer to God will usually enlarge your gift's operation.

c. Character - We shall be like Him someday – but the work starts now.

d. The right balance is to be happy with whom we are and where we are in the Lord right now, while still pressing forward toward the goal of excellence. **Phil 3:10-14**

HOW DOES GOD PREPARE YOU FOR YOUR SPECIFIC MINISTRY?

What is God doing in your life? Have you found a place to serve and a place of ministry within the Kingdom of God? What are some principles for how God prepares you for your place of ministry?

1. **By Sitting - Lk. 10:38-42**

   a. Being before Doing

      i. Your relationship to God is the starting point for all ministry.

      ii. Being must come before any doing is possible.

   b. Waiting before Producing

      i. God is more interested in who you are in him than in what you can do for him.

      ii. It took 80 years for Moses to be…

      iii. It only took one burning bush to catapult him into his ministry.

      iv. It took 30 years for Joseph to be….

      v. It only took a shave and fresh clothes to put him in his ministry.

   c. God's preparation of a leader involves training, extended times of waiting, pain, rejection, refining and isolation. Moses was brought up in Pharaoh's court. He had the very best of everything; education, clothing, food, and personal care. But there came a time when the man God would use to free an entire nation from slavery was going to have to learn to be the leader God wanted. At the age of 40 Moses was forced to flee to the desert.

   Like Abraham, Joseph, David and Paul, Moses had to endure some difficult years of preparation that first involved being removed from his current situation. He went from notoriety to obscurity, from limitless resources to no resources, from activity and action to inactivity and solitude. And, most importantly, waiting. And waiting. And more waiting. He probably thought he would die on the back side of the desert.

Then one day, a full 40 years from the day he arrived, God appeared to Moses in a burning bush. In a moment everything changed. God said, "It is time." The years had seasoned the man to prepare him to accomplish the work.

God is preparing many leaders today. The circumstances may be different. The time frames may not be quite as long. But the characteristics of the training are still the same. Do not try to shortcut the desert time of God. It only leads to cul-de-sacs, which force you to revisit the lessons you were meant to learn. Embrace them, so that He can use your life for something extraordinary.

2. By Serving - Mk. 10:42-45

a. Once a basic relationship has been formed between you and Jesus then you should get involved. All have been called to general involvement.

The *Whatever* Principle

Ps. 1:1-3 - If a man delights in God then *whatever* they do will prosper

Eccl. 9:10 - *Whatever* your hand finds to do

Col. 3:23-24 - *Whatever* you do - work at it with all your heart

Albert Switzer was once asked if he had found happiness in Africa and he replied, "I have found a place to serve, that's enough happiness for anyone."

3. By Seeking Guidance - Heb. 13:17

a. Constantly remember to **ask God first**, then be open to see where God is leading you.

b. **Listen** to the comments and opinions of leaders as they can give you their insight into your own abilities and areas of effectiveness. A prophecy given to you personally may confirm an area of calling. *Be teachable! Be submissive!*

4. Through Sober Self-Evaluation - Rom. 12:3

a. Consider your natural abilities and desires. You should evaluate your talents and realistically determine for what you are qualified. A person who is tone deaf is probably not called to be a worship leader. A person who is easily irritated by children ought not to be involved with kids.

b. God's grace energizes your natural abilities. Strong and consistent desire may also indicate a calling to a specific area of ministry.

1 Cor. 12:31 - *eagerly desire the greater gifts-NIV Earnestly desire the best gifts-NKJ*

c. If you have persistent itch that will not go away - scratch it!

5. By Studying - 2 Tim. 2:15

a. Even after you discover a place of ministry and function you must be diligent and continue to prepare yourself.

b. **2 Tim. 2:15** KJV - *study* = to make effort, labor   NIV – do your best

6. By Sacrificing - Lk. 14:26-27

a. You cannot stay where you are and do the ministry God has for you. There is a cost with every calling in the kingdom. The Lord tests your commitment and motives by your willingness to sacrificially apply yourself.

b. Someone once said that you can tell the genuineness of someone's ministry if they are willing to pay you to let them do it.

HOW CAN GODLY CONDUCT BE DEVELOPED?

ACTS 20:17-31

*17 From Miletus, Paul sent to Ephesus for the **elders** of the church. 18 When they arrived, he said to them: "You know how I lived the whole time I was with you, from the first day I came into the province of Asia. 19 I served the Lord with great humility and with tears, although I was severely tested by the plots of the Jews. 20 You know that I have not hesitated to preach anything that would be helpful to you but have taught you publicly and from house to house. 21 I have declared to both Jews and Greeks that they must turn to God in repentance and have faith in our Lord Jesus.*

22 "And now, compelled by the Spirit, I am going to Jerusalem, not knowing what will happen to me there. 23 I only know that in every city the Holy Spirit warns me that prison and hardships are facing me. 24 However, I consider my life worth nothing to me, if only I may finish the race and complete the task the Lord Jesus has given me — the task of testifying to the gospel of God's grace.

25 "Now I know that none of you among whom I have gone about preaching the kingdom will ever see me again. 26 Therefore, I declare to you today that I am innocent of the blood of all men. 27 For I have not hesitated to proclaim to you the whole will of

*God. 28 Keep watch over yourselves and all the flock of which the Holy Spirit has made you **overseers**. Be **shepherds** of the church of God, which he bought with his own blood. 29 I know that after I leave, savage wolves will come in among you and will not spare the flock. 30 Even from your own number men will arise and distort the truth in order to draw away disciples after them. 31 So be on your guard! Remember that for three years I never stopped warning each of you night and day with tears.*

In this passage we see that the Apostle Paul is returning to Jerusalem and in order to save time he bypasses the city of Ephesus, but then calls the Elders of the church to come to him in Miletus. Here he addresses the leaders of the church and makes several strong points about how they, as Elders and Shepherds should conduct themselves.

In this farewell speech Paul's topics can basically be broken down into three categories.

1. How to personally be pleasing to God - Keep watch over yourselves - v. 28

2. How to deal with wolves - Keep watching for wolves' vv. 29-30

3. How to shepherd the sheep - Keep watch over the flock - v. 28

I. HOW TO BE PERSONALLY PLEASING TO GOD

Acts 20:28- *Keep watch over yourselves* and all the flock of which the Holy Spirit has made you overseers. Be shepherds of the church of God, which he bought with his own blood.

In looking at Paul's first topic, keeping watch over yourselves, this can readily be seen to apply to how a leader should conduct themselves so that they are personally pleasing to God.

In **1 Timothy 4**, Paul gives instruction to his young disciple about the defining characteristics of a Godly leader and uses the same term that he used for the Ephesian elders when he said to 'keep watch' over yourselves in **Acts 20:28**, and so he ties the two passages together. In **1 Tim. 4:16** he exhorts Timothy to "Watch your life and doctrine closely." If that is Paul's conclusion, then what was the context?

In **1 Timothy 4:7**, Paul tells Timothy that he must *train himself to be Godly.*

1. **How do you train yourself to be a godly leader?**

    1 Timothy 4:7 - *Have nothing to do with godless myths and old wives' tales; rather, train yourself to be godly.*

a. You can train yourself to be godly through discipline.

Discipline is defined by the *Merriam-Webster Dictionary* as "training that corrects, molds, or perfects the mental faculties or moral character." It is a type of training that involves intentionally delaying short-term benefits for a long-term good. After catching his student asleep at his half-finished statue, the Italian painter Bertoldo once said to Michelangelo, "Talent is cheap; discipline is everything."

Hebrews 12:1-3 - You can finish the race of faith by *throwing off* sin, *running* with endurance, *fixing your eyes* on Jesus, *considering him,* and by *not growing weary!*

2 Peter 1:3-8 -You need discipline (self-control and perseverance) to be effective and productive in your faith. This is an absolute necessity in the conduct of a leader.

2 Kings 2:7-10 - Elisha received a double portion from Elijah by persistence and discipline.

b. You can train yourself to be godly through prayer.

Prayer is an absolutely essential facet of the Christian life. Paul wrote "Pray continually" **1 Thess. 5:17**.

Luke 18:1 - Never give up in prayer, breakthrough is closer than you think!

Matthew 18:19 - There is power in agreement. Whether it is spouses, or simply two individuals agreeing together, there is great effectiveness in this type of prayer.

Ps. 63:1 - Earnestly I seek you - David's heart song should be yours as well.

Isa. 26:8-9 - My soul yearns for you in the night - Isaiah was also a man of prayer.

c. You can train yourself to be godly through Bible-reading.

In **Matthew 4:4** when Jesus said, *Man does not live on bread alone, but on every word that comes from the mouth of God,* He was saying even more than by food, people must be daily sustained by the word of God. There is a strong case to be made not just for daily Bible reading, but for reading through the entire Bible regularly, perhaps on a yearly basis.

Jeremiah 15:16 - "When your words came, I ate them; they were my joy and my heart's delight..."

2 Timothy 3:14-16 "...from infancy you have known the holy Scriptures, which are able to make you wise for salvation..."

Hebrews 5:12-14 - Simply reading the Bible is good, but you also must be trained in it, and use it to train yourself to distinguish good from evil.

d.   You can train yourself to be godly through submission.

God's vision for His church is that it might be organized and led by those He appoints. You are to not only worship God, but also honor and submit to those He has chosen to lead. **Ephesians 4:7-12** gives a glimpse of how Christ set up His Church. Verse seven speaks of how He gave grace (Gr: *charis*) to each one of us. **Eph. 4:11** lists the types of ministers He gave at His ascension to equip His people.

   Apostles - For fathering.

   Prophets - For directing.

   Evangelists - For birthing.

   Pastors - For caring.

   Teachers - For instructing.

Finally in verse twelve it says that the reason He gave these ministries was to prepare God's people for works of service. Leaders in the church pray and minister the word, which is how they train the body; preparing God's people so that everyone can be fruitful in their God-given ministries.

Acts 6:1-4 - The apostles approved of the men chosen to serve who were "known to be full of the Spirit and wisdom." These men had been trained already! They gave themselves to serving while the apostles gave themselves to ministry. Then God moved some of the seven into other ministries. Stephen would go on to preach in Jerusalem and become the first martyr, Acts 6:8 - 7:60. Philip would become an evangelist, preaching the word in Samaria and seeing many notable miracles, **Acts 8:4-40; 21:8-9**.

2 Timothy 2:2 – *And the things you have heard me say in the presence of many witnesses entrust to reliable men who will also be qualified to teach others.*

In this one verse, four "generations" of ministers are mentioned. Paul training Timothy, and then Timothy training others who could train others as well. The act of training/equipping/entrusting implies submission by the trainee.

2. **According to Paul in 1 Tim. 4:9-12, in what areas do leaders need to be an example?**

   1 Timothy 4:9-12 - *This is a trustworthy saying that deserves full acceptance (and for this we labor and strive), that we have put our hope in the living God, who is the Savior of all men, and especially of those who believe. Command and teach these things. Don't let anyone look down on you because you are young, but set an example for the believers in speech, in life, in love, (* NKJ here has 'spirit') in faith and in purity.*

   a. *Speech* - Leaders need to watch their words so carefully. **Ephesians 4:29** says your words must not be "unwholesome" but should only be used if they are "helpful for building others up."

   b. *Life* - The way a leader conducts every area of their life must be an example. Paul was able to say confidently "Follow me as I follow Christ." **1 Corinthians 11:1**

   c. *Love* - The most important thing that a leader, or anyone, can do is express love Biblically, **1 Corinthians 13**. Love fulfills the entire law **Luke 10:27**.

   d. *Spirit* - **See Romans 12:11**. A leader must be an example by maintaining "spiritual fervor."

   e. *Faith* - If a leader is not an example of faith, where else will the people see it? See Mark 11:22-24 and Hebrews 11:6.

   f. *Purity* - See **Titus 1:15-16**. Leaders must be an example of purity in word, thought, and deed. **1 Peter 1:22** says purity comes through obedience. **1 Peter 1:13-15** is not just a command to leaders, but to all: "Be holy in all you do."

3. **To what should leaders devote themselves?**

   1 Timothy 4:13 - *Until I come, devote yourself to the public reading of Scripture, to preaching and to teaching.*

   a. *Publicly reading the Scripture.* Sounds simple, unless of course you can't read. I was once asked what the number one requirement for being a pastor was. I quickly replied, the ability to read. Reading, studying, preparing for teaching and preaching all rests on this ability. I am sure that any exceptions to my requirement find themselves extremely handicapped in ministry. If one feels called by God to Pastor then, no matter their age or capability, they should pursue learning to read and write.

   b. *Preaching* - Preaching has to do with exhortation. The Greek word means to proclaim the word, as a herald. In **2 Timothy 4:2**, Paul again challenged Timothy to

"Preach the Word!" If you read **1 Pet. 4:10-11** you'll see that as a preacher, you are God's spokesman. I will cover this topic more in detail later.

c. *Teaching* - Teaching has to do with doctrine, taking people from the unknown into the known. **Hebrews 5:11-14** talks about how spiritual babies need milk-simple elementary teachings. **Acts 8:30-31** says that understanding comes as a result of teaching. In the Old Testament, in **Nehemiah 8:7-8**, the Levites instructed the people and helped them to understand the meaning of the Word by making it clear.

4. **How can a leader make sure they are not neglecting their gift?**

   1 Timothy 4:14 - *Do not neglect the gift that is in you, which was given to you by prophecy with the laying on of the hands of the eldership.* NKJV

   a. A person's gift is simply the thing that God has enabled you to be good at. A leader must recognize what they are good at, and enjoy it!

   b. **2 Timothy 1:6** says that a gift must be fanned into flame, giving the illustration of a gift as fire. This is a reference to the Old Testament when God would give holy fire to burn at the Tabernacle (**Numbers 27:22-23, Deu. 34:9, Acts 13:3**). See also **1 Timothy 1:18**.

   c. A gift once given then becomes the receiver's responsibility. It is up to you whether you use the gift on a regular basis, by stirring it up, or let it become dormant even to the point of dying out like an ember.

5. **How does a leader constantly maintain diligence?**

   1 Timothy 4:15-16 - *Give your complete attention to these matters. Throw yourself into your tasks so that everyone will see your progress. 16 Keep a close watch on how you live and on your teaching. Stay true to what is right for the sake of your own salvation and the salvation of those who hear you.* NLT

   a. In addition to constantly walking in discipline and self-control, it is necessary to have a goal. Jesus was able to endure the cross because he had a goal, "the joy set before him..." **Hebrews 12:2**. In **Philippians 4:10-14**, Paul speaks of how his goal was "to win the prize" for which God called him heavenward.

   b. An interesting thought out of **1 Tim. 4:15** comes with the word "progress". The Greek definition has to do with 'chopping that which is ahead, a driving forward.' It can be today be used for 'the cutting edge'. If you will throw yourself into your task then you can remain on the cutting edge of your ministry.

II. HOW TO DEAL WITH WOLVES

CHARACTERISTICS OF WOLVES

Acts 20:29-31 - *I know that after I leave, savage wolves will come in among you and will not spare the flock. Even from your own number men will arise and distort the truth in order to draw away disciples after them. So be on your guard! Remember that for three years I never stopped warning each of you night and day with tears.*

In this portion of scripture, Paul warns the elders at Ephesus about the fact that wolves would rise up to attempt to devour the sheep of the flock. Jesus had prophesied this when he told his disciples "I am sending you out like sheep among wolves." (Matthew 10:16). Jesus also gave this warning.

Matt 7:15-20 - *"Watch out for false prophets. They come to you in sheep's clothing, but inwardly they are ferocious wolves. By their fruit you will recognize them. Do people pick grapes from thorn bushes, or figs from thistles? Likewise every good tree bears good fruit, but a bad tree bears bad fruit. A good tree cannot bear bad fruit, and a bad tree cannot bear good fruit. Every tree that does not bear good fruit is cut down and thrown into the fire. Thus, by their fruit you will recognize them.*

I can clearly see that God is moving around the world. In country after country the church is exploding with new believers. From what I read and experience it seems that currently there is someone being born into the Kingdom of God at a rate of one every two seconds. Praise God for that as it's nothing short of miraculous. Yet with this increase of "lambs" there is a corresponding increase in predators – or wolves! In the New Testament writers frequently warned of wolves, or false ministers of God, who would try to wreak havoc with the church. Jesus said that by their fruit you will recognize them. Let's look at several passages that describe the characteristics of **false minsters** and then compare and contrast those characteristics to Paul's clear description of **wolves** in Acts 20.

False apostles are spoken of in **2 Corinthians 10:12, 11:13-15** and **20**.

2 Cor. 10:12 - *We do not dare to classify or compare ourselves with some who commend themselves. When they measure themselves by themselves and compare themselves with themselves, they are not wise.*

2 Cor. 11:13-15 - *For such men are false apostles, deceitful workmen, masquerading as apostles of Christ. And no wonder, for Satan himself masquerades as an angel of light. It is not*

43

surprising, then, if his servants masquerade as servants of righteousness. Their end will be what their actions deserve.

2 Cor. 11:20-21 - *In fact, you even put up with anyone who enslaves you or exploits you or takes advantage of you or pushes himself forward or slaps you in the face.*

The coming of **false prophets** is foretold in **2 Peter 2:1-3** and **10-14**.

2 Peter 2:1-3 - *But there were also false prophets among the people, just as there will be false teachers among you. They will secretly introduce destructive heresies, even denying the sovereign Lord who bought them — bringing swift destruction on themselves. Many will follow their shameful ways and will bring the way of truth into disrepute. In their greed these teachers will exploit you with stories they have made up. Their condemnation has long been hanging over them, and their destruction has not been sleeping.*

2 Peter 2:10-15 - *This is especially true of those who follow the corrupt desire of the sinful nature and despise authority. Bold and arrogant, these men are not afraid to slander celestial beings; yet even angels, although they are stronger and more powerful, do not bring slanderous accusations against such beings in the presence of the Lord. But these men blaspheme in matters they do not understand. They are like brute beasts, creatures of instinct, born only to be caught and destroyed, and like beasts they too will perish. They will be paid back with harm for the harm they have done. Their idea of pleasure is to carouse in broad daylight. They are blots and blemishes, reveling in their pleasures while they feast with you. With eyes full of adultery, they never stop sinning; they seduce the unstable; they are experts in greed — an accursed brood!*

False teachers and shepherds are mentioned in **Jude 1:4, 8-13**, and **16-19**.

Jude 1:3-4 - *Dear friends, although I was very eager to write to you about the salvation we share, I felt I had to write and urge you to contend for the faith that was once for all entrusted to the saints. For certain men whose condemnation was written about long ago have secretly slipped in among you. They are godless men, who change the grace of our God into a license for immorality and deny Jesus Christ our only Sovereign and Lord.*

Jude 1:8-13 - *In the very same way, these dreamers pollute their own bodies, reject authority and slander celestial beings. But even the archangel Michael, when he was disputing with the devil about the body of Moses, did not dare to bring a slanderous accusation against him, but said, "The Lord rebuke you!" Yet these men speak abusively against whatever they do not understand; and what things they do understand by instinct, like unreasoning animals — these are the very things that destroy* *them. Woe to them! They have taken the way of Cain; they have rushed for profit into Balaam's error; they have been destroyed in Korah's rebellion. These men are blemishes at your love feasts, eating with you without the slightest qualm — shepherds who feed only themselves. They are clouds without rain, blown along by the wind; autumn trees, without fruit and uprooted — twice dead. They are wild waves of the sea, foaming up their shame; wandering stars, for whom blackest darkness has been reserved forever.*

1. **How will wolves treat the flock?**

   Acts 20:29 - *I know that after I leave, savage wolves will come in among you and will not spare the flock.*

   Wolves "will not spare the flock." Wolves will use the sheep to satisfy their own desires.

   a. **They will enslave them - 2 Corinthians 11:20**. They come to enslave not to serve.

   b. **They will exploit them - 2 Corinthians 11:20**. **2 Peter 2:3** says they will exploit people by telling stories that they have made up.

   c. **They will take advantage of them** - This is another quote from **2 Cor. 11:20**.

   d. **They will only feed themselves** - Perhaps the greatest indictment against these false teachers is that though they occupy a position that is meant to be all about providing for others, they, in the words of Jude, "feed only themselves." **Jude 1:12**

2. **Where will the wolves come from?**

   Acts 20:30 - *Even from your own number men will arise and distort the truth in order to draw away disciples after them.*

   Wolves will come from within the Church, or as Paul said, "Even from your own number." Their threat comes from their influence. A wolf must try to become a leader, otherwise they pose little threat to the sheep. That is why Pastors/Shepherds must be so very careful and know those who labor with them among the sheep. Now wolves are born wolves and sheep are born sheep, but sheep (Shepherds) can take on wolfish characteristics. These wolfish characteristics can and must be repented of for ongoing effective ministry.

   a. **They masquerade as apostles** - In **2 Corinthians 11:13-15**, Paul calls the false apostles "deceitful workmen." He compares their masquerade to the way Satan pretends to be an angel of light. Wolves rarely change. Jesus said that a bad tree cannot bear good fruit.

Deluded and deceived followers of wolves might take on the characteristics of a wolf but still have the ability to repent and change. Wolves are wolves and rarely repent.

b. **They are "blots and blemishes"** - This is a quote from **2 Peter 2:13** describing how the wolves feast among the believers, yet don't quite fit in.

c. **They secretly slip in among you - Jude 1:4**. Wolves are not always obvious, this is why it is important to be on the lookout for them. In Biblical times wolves could easily slip in among a flock of sheep if the shepherd was not careful. From a distance they looked similar. The stood about the same height and except for their pointed ears they could easily be overlooked. The closer a shepherd got, though, the easier it was to detect the wolf.

3. **What will the wolves teach?**

Acts 20:30 - *Even from your own number men will arise and distort the truth in order to draw away disciples after them.*

Paul said that the wolves would "distort the truth". They may not always make up obvious lies, but they will intentionally twist the truth in subtle ways. They will especially take the words of the Shepherd and twist them and distort them, all with the intent of drawing sheep closer for their attack.

a. **They are deceitful - 2 Corinthians 11:13**. Though they tell lies, they make it sound like the truth. God's people must be on their guard like the Bereans were, as they "examined the Scriptures every day to see if what Paul said was true." **Acts 17:11**

b. **They teach destructive heresies - 2 Peter 2:1**. "The thief comes to steal, kill, and destroy..." **Jn. 10:10**. The lies of a wolf are damaging and destructive.

c. **They seduce the unstable - 2 Peter 2:14**. Wolves prey on the unstable, those who are easily attracted by shallow pleasures and persuasive speech.

d. **They are experts in greed - 2 Peter 1:14**. Wolves are often skilled at managing money and acquiring it for themselves. See the example of Judas in John 12:6. In the church today is this not part of what a wolf is actually seeking?

4. **What are wolves ultimately after?**

Acts 20:30 - *Even from your own number men will arise and distort the truth in order to draw away disciples after them.*

Wolves are power hungry. In the end of **Acts 20:30**, Paul says that their ultimate goal is to "draw away disciples after themselves."

a. **They push themselves forward - 2 Corinthians 11:20**. Rather than waiting for God to promote them or advance them, they take matters into their own hands, knowing that if they don't do this it won't happen.

b. **They compare and commend themselves - 2 Corinthians 10:12, Jude 1:16, 2 Peter 2:10**. Instead of finding their identity in what God says about them, wolves need to validate themselves by making themselves look better than others. It's all about them. Be very cautious of a leader who is always comparing themselves to other leaders especially in a self-effacing way. Their false modesty ought to be a dead giveaway.

c. **They despise authority - 2 Peter 2:10, Jude 1:18**. Wolves do not know how to be truly humble. Though they may wait in a position of submission for a time, they will resent it in their hearts and bide their time until it's time to strike.

d. **They are grumblers and faultfinders - Jude 1:16**. Whereas for believers, "love covers" (**1 Peter 4:8**), wolves delight in exposing the flaws of others.

e. **They cause divisions - Jude 1:19**. Wolves try to lead people away from the established vision of the house. Division simply means "two-visions."

f. **They have eyes full of adultery - 2 Peter 2:14** - Wolves are driven by base, fleshly passions. Though they don't always act on impulse immediately, they are always looking for opportunities.

III. HOW TO SHEPHERD THE SHEEP

Acts 20:28 - *"Keep watch over yourselves and all the flock of which the Holy Spirit has made you overseers. Be shepherds of the church of God, which he bought with his own blood."* NIV

THE CONDUCT OF SHEPHERDS

Now that we've examined the threat that wolves pose to the people of God, we can look at the shepherds, the people that God has placed in his body to protect the flock. The picture of God's people as a flock of sheep is a reoccurring theme throughout scripture. Here we are going to look at the Biblical characteristics of shepherds.

1. **What does Ezekiel 34:4, 16 teach us about a shepherd's ministry?**

   4 You have not strengthened the weak or healed the sick or bound up the injured. You have not brought back the strays or searched for the lost. You have ruled them harshly and

47

*brutally. **16** I will search for the lost and bring back the strays. I will bind up the injured and strengthen the weak, but the sleek and the strong I will destroy. I will shepherd the flock with justice.*

A natural shepherd's job was to:

a. **Strengthen the weak** through proper diet and exercise. Leading the sheep to green pasture is not just a euphemism. Left to themselves sheep will stay in one location, eventually ruin the land by overgrazing and then pollute it to their own detriment. Sheep must be led to green pastures regularly.

b. **Heal the sick** by caring for their practical needs. A shepherd usually carried a bag within which were items to care for the sick. Cloth to bind the wound and anointing oil to spread over the wound to help the healing process. Without the watchful eye of the shepherd a sheep could injure himself which if not cared for could prove fatal.

c. **Bring back the strays** by whatever means necessary. A shepherd would sometimes need to break a sheep's leg in order to prevent the sheep from wandering. Once the shepherd resorted to this extreme measure he would have to carry that sheep on his shoulders until the broken leg healed. In the process that sheep would bond with the shepherd and once healed, never again leave the shepherd's side.

d. **Seek the lost** with intentional effort. Some sheep accidently stray looking for green pasture while others do it habitually, always looking for the grass on the other side of the fence. In **Luke 15:3-7** this is perfectly illustrated by Jesus' parable of the Lost Sheep.

e. **Rule them without harshness or brutality**. Speaks of leading by inspiration, not force. Literally the word 'harshly' means to break apart, fracture and speaks of severity. The word 'brutality' means vehemence, from the word for power in a negative sense, or to fasten upon, to seize. Here the Great Shepherd is challenging the undersheperds to never resort to these means of leading the flock.

2. **What does Matthew 2:6 teach us about shepherding?**

Matt. 2:6 - "'But you, Bethlehem, in the land of Judah, are by no means least among the rulers of Judah; for out of you will come a ruler who will be the shepherd of my people Israel.'"

It was prophesied (originally in Micah 5:2) that Jesus would be a shepherd for the people of Israel. The word 'ruler' in

48

the NIV means to lead, to command. KJV translates it 'governor'. The word for shepherd is 'poimaino' which emphasizes the feeding aspect of watching the flock. That meant the ruler would be responsible for feeding the people. A pastor's right to lead is based on his ability to feed the sheep.

3. **What can we learn about being a shepherd from Psalm 23?**

   1 The LORD is my shepherd, I lack nothing. 2 He makes me lie down in green pastures, he leads me beside quiet waters, 3 he refreshes my soul. He guides me along the right paths for his name's sake. 4 Even though I walk through the darkest valley, I will fear no evil, for you are with me; your rod and your staff, they comfort me. 5 You prepare a table before me in the presence of my enemies. You anoint my head with oil; my cup overflows. 6 Surely your goodness and love will follow me all the days of my life, and I will dwell in the house of the LORD forever.

   a. **v.2. He makes me lie down.** There are three requirements that must be met before the sheep are able to lie down in peace.

      i. They must be free from fear of wolves

      ii. They must be free from torment from pests

      iii. They must be free from bullies (older sheep who like to butt heads.)

      iv. All of these requirements can only be met if the shepherd is doing his job. The shepherd is the one who sees, discerns and fights the wolves. Knowledge of the shepherd's presence allows the sheep to lie down. Only the shepherd can free the sheep from the torment of pests. He reaches into his bag and uses the anointing oil (which was a natural bug repellent) to anoint the sheep's' head with oil. Only with that oil could the sheep lie down and be free from pests. And then the bullies, who are more afraid of the shepherd and his staff than the need to assert themselves and bully the young and tender lambs. The knowledge that the shepherd is nearby prevents the head-butting that is a constant with his presence.

   b. **v.2. In green pastures.** The shepherd provides pastures of tender grass, or good food!

      i. Rich food comes through study and preparation.

      ii. Most pastors only have three sermons, they just

present them in different ways.

iii. In order for the sheep in every church to experience green pastures the shepherd must constantly be watching (studying and preparing) for the green pastures. A great recommendation for all pastors is that a preaching calendar be kept. This calendar is *prayerfully* created to help the pastor make sure he doesn't resort to plucking his same two strings on his banjo, which seems to be a natural tendency. The calendar can help remind the shepherd of what has been preached and then what needs to be preached to insure a healthy diet. This does not preclude the moving of the Spirit, but rather insures that green pastures are available.

c. **vv.2-3. He leads, guides, and restores.**

i. The shepherd doesn't lead towards turbulent waters, but to quiet waters; not into controversy, but sound doctrine. A church going through a split is one turbulent place! At those times the sheep can never find rest. A pastor who loves to stir the pot and keep things exciting sometimes doesn't realize the negative impact turbulence can have long term on the sheep.

ii. The shepherd guides the sheep to paths of righteousness; different and good paths. The Hebrew word for guide means to lead, to transport, to colonize. The shepherd is consciously taking the sheep from where they have been to a place where they need to be, the right path, the path of righteousness.

iii. The good shepherd restores the sheep. The NIV uses the word 'refreshes'. The Hebrew word means to turn back, generally to retreat. One of the best ways to get the sheep to constantly turn back or retreat is through the concept of the regular Sabbath. The Sabbath was given so that man could rest from his labors. This weekly rest was meant to be a time of refreshing of both body, soul and spirit.

d. **v.4. He is with them -** Wherever and whenever.

i. His rod is for protection, a weapon against wolves.

ii. His staff is for correction, to direct the sheep

when they stray from the right path.

    iii.   Both tools ultimately bring comfort to the sheep because they know that the shepherd has everything under control.

  e. **v.5. He prepares a table before them.** This could refer to the "table-land," high fields filled with rich grass. The shepherd is leading the sheep to a place of rich fulfillment.

  f. **v.6. He anoints my head with oil.** As mentioned above, the shepherd would pour oil over the heads of the sheep to keep pests away from their eyes, nose, and mouth. It protected them from distractions and annoyances.

4. **What did Peter learn about the importance of shepherding?**

Peter's Denial and Restoration

John 18:12-14 - On the night he was betrayed Jesus is taken first to Annas, then to Caiphas.

Luke 22:54-62 - In Luke's description of Peter denying his relationship with Jesus, at one point Jesus looks upon him. It is most likely at the time when Jesus is being transferred from Annas to Caiphas as mentioned in John's account. Then we see Peter recognizing his own failure and begins to weep.

John 21:15-17 - After the resurrection, Jesus asks Peter to affirm his love three times to make up for the three denials. In turn Jesus exhorted Peter three times, saying "feed my sheep." Jesus' reinstatement of Peter was for the expressed purpose of feeding the sheep!

5. **What did Peter say about the perils and privileges of pastoring in 1 Peter 5:1-4?**

*To the **elders** among you, I appeal as a fellow elder, a witness of Christ's sufferings and one who also will share in the glory to be revealed: 2 Be **shepherds** of God's flock that is under your care, serving as **overseers** — not because you must, but because you are willing, as God wants you to be; not greedy for money, but eager to serve; 3 not lording it over those entrusted to you, but being examples to the flock. 4 And when the Chief Shepherd appears, you will receive the crown of glory that will never fade away.*

1 Peter 5:1-4 - Addressed to the leaders of the church but using three Greek words

    Presbuteros = Elders – a title saying who they are – v.1

    Episkopos = Overseer – saying what they do – v. 2

    Poimaino = Shepherds – saying how they do it – v. 2

Archipoimen - Jesus is the Chief Shepherd – v. 4.

All Pastors and Leaders are under Christ's authority.

Luke 7:1-9 - The Centurion was a man under authority. He had great faith due to his understanding of authority. As you submit to authority you can function with great faith as well!

a. **Peril #1 – Lack of Desire**

Not by constraint – NIV "not because you must"

Moses – Ex. 4:13 – please send someone else

Gideon – Jud. 6:13 – But if the Lord is with us why then….

b. **Peril #2 – A Desire for Gain**

Not for filthy lucre – not greedy for money

Yet this could also mean any type of gain that would feed someone's selfish desires. **2 Kin. 5:1-27 – Naaman, Elisha, Gehazi**

c. **Peril #3 – A Desire for Power**

Not lording it over those entrusted to you

This speaks of domineering or high-handed rule

3 Jn. 1:9-11 – Diotrephes loves to be first

d. **Privilege #1 – Serving with Zeal**

v. 2 – *but because you are willing* - From 2 Grk words; forward and spirit, and so – serving with zeal - It is a privilege to serve the King by serving others!

Rom. 12:11 – NIV – Never be lacking in zeal, but keep your spiritual fervor, serving the Lord.

e. **Privilege #2 – Serving with Enthusiasm**

v.2 – *but eager to serve*

With energy and enthusiasm for the job

Col. 3:22-24 – with all your heart - **Enthusiasm = God-inside-mindedness**

f. **Privilege #3 – Serving as Examples**

v.3 – *but being examples to the flock*

Greek - a type, a die (as struck); a stamp or scar

From the root word - to thump, cudgel or pummel.

Elder's or Leader's lives illustrate the thumping that produces a Divine stamp or scar.

g. **The Chief Pastor/Shepherd**

v.4 – *And when the Chief Shepherd appears*

Chief Shepherd- "This phrase delicately reminds the elders that they are His delegates, and hints at His right to call them to account and, if appropriate, reward them."

receive - This term is often used for receiving pay or wages. Here it is speaking of eternal rewards received on judgment day.

never fade away - The crown promised to obedient elders/leaders is not like the ones won in the games - of leaves or branches. This crown will never wither or fade.

HOW SHOULD GOD'S CHURCH BE GOVERNED?

1. **What system of government did the Apostles establish over the churches?**

   Acts 14:23 – *Paul and Barnabas appointed elders for them in each church and, with prayer and fasting, committed them to the Lord, in whom they had put their trust.*

   Paul appointed Elders in the churches, after only a 3 month trip! How could this be? Today it seems like it can take us years to produce someone of character and integrity qualified to be an Elder. The key is that Paul was dealing with the Jewish system and synagogues. The Jews in the Old Testament had always had Elders. So it seems that the Apostles were able to appoint Elders in every city because in character and conduct there were no doubt Elders already functioning within the synagogues. They simply needed their Content – or Doctrine – adjusted with the news about the Messiah – He had come and His name was Jesus!

   Ex. 18:12 - Moses and the elders, here probably the older men, met with Jethro.

   Ex. 18:13-26 - Jethro imparts wisdom, Moses listens and makes leaders, who probably became the 'Elders' within the nation. Verse 21 states their qualifications; capable, in fear of God, trustworthy, and full of integrity.

2. **What terms are used in the New Testament to describe the leaders of the church?**

   Acts 20:17, 28 –

   *17 From Miletus, Paul sent to Ephesus for the **elders** of the church.*

   *28 Keep watch over yourselves and all the flock of which the Holy Spirit has made you **overseers**. Be **shepherds** of the* *church of God, which he bought with his own blood.*

The following three words refer to the same position in the church.

Presbuteros	=	Older vs. 17
Episkopos	=	Overseer vs. 28
Poimaino	=	Pastor vs. 28 – from the Greek

word 'to feed'

1 Pet. 5:1-4 –

*To the **elders** among you, I appeal as a fellow elder, a witness of Christ's sufferings and one who also will share in the glory to be revealed: 2 Be **shepherds** of God's flock that is under your care, serving as **overseers** — not because you must, but because you are willing, as God wants you to be; not greedy for money, but eager to serve; 3 not lording it over those entrusted to you, but being examples to the flock. 4 And when the Chief Shepherd appears, you will receive the crown of glory that will never fade away.*

Peter uses these same three words to describe the leaders of God's flock.

Presbuteros	=	Older vs. 1
Poimaino	=	Pastor - Shepherd vs. 2
Episkopos	=	Overseer - watching over them vs. 2

3. **What are the main principles about Elders governing the church?**

There is no indication of a position higher than Elder in the New Testament. Our commonly used term Bishop (1 Tim. 3:1 in the KJV), comes from the term *episkopos*, which was a local church office, not a position above or controlling the local church.

There are people of experience who give good advice to churches, but the elders are responsible before God for the leadership of the local church. They may seek advice from people of experience, but the advice is not directive.

Most churches have a pastor in the leading position. They are the leading Elder among a group of equals (first among equals).

The position we refer to as pastor is neither superior to nor inferior to an Elder, but is simply a way in which we maintain good order and accountability in the church.

4. **What are the Biblical areas of responsibility for an Elder?**

There are six main areas of responsibility for Elders.

a. **Elders lead, or govern, the church, guided by the Holy Spirit**

The following scriptures refer to a leadership role for the Elders (and apostles, whom I consider to also be Elders of the church). **Acts 15:4, 6, 22, 23; 16:4**

The Greek word *proistemi* means to lead. **Rom 12:8, 1 Thess. 5:12, 1 Tim. 3:4-5, 5:17**

The term Elder is almost always found in the plural form, indicating that the church is not governed by a single Elder, but rather a group of Elders. **Acts 20:17-18, 21:18, Jas. 5:14**

The scriptures show that there is a leading Elder. **Acts 15:13, 19.**

Peter and John refer to themselves as Elders rather than as apostles. This may be because they considered the apostle's ministry (and perhaps all of the ministry gifts of Ephesians 4:11) to include an implied Elder ministry. **1 Pet 5:1, 2 John 1, 3 John 1**

The priority of the leading Elder is in teaching, though all the Elders are supposed to be able to teach. **1 Tim. 5:17.**

Acts 15 shows how important matters are handled.

Not directly with the church v. 6

According to the scriptures v. 15

According to the Spirit v. 28

Elders should seek the guidance of scripture and the confirmation of the Holy Spirit in their decisions.

Governing the church involves overseeing the finances. **Acts 4:37; 11:29-30**

b. **Elders are the shepherds for God's flock**

Elders are pastors, even if they are not the lead pastor of the church, and should act accordingly. **Acts 20:28, 1 Peter 5:2**

A shepherd goes before the flock, that is, they are an example to the people in prayer, character, willingness to serve, the study of scripture, good works, etc. **1 Peter 5:3**

A shepherd/pastor loves the sheep. It should be evident in their behavior **John 10:11**

A shepherd/pastor watches over the spiritual lives of the people. **Heb. 13:17**

A shepherd/pastor discerns prophecy, teaching, and all

other activities in the church. They are responsible that things are done in ways that glorify God. **1 Corinthians 14:29**

c. **Elders preach and teach**

Elders are responsible for preaching and teaching. **1 Tim. 3:2, 1 Tim. 5:17, Acts 6:4**

They lead people to good (spiritual) pasture. **Ephesians 4:11, Psalm 23**

They know the scriptures and are able to establish sound doctrine. **2 Tim. 4:3-4**

They represent God in the congregation. So they don't teach their own opinions, but rather what God intends for the church. **2 Tim. 4:2, 1 Pet. 4:10-11**

d. **Elders correct, rebuke and encourage**

They do these things with great patience. **2 Tim. 4:2**

They warn with tears, which imply a full emotional involvement. **Acts 20:31**

They base their encouragement and correction on the word of God. **Titus 1:9**

They administer church discipline. **1 Cor. 5:3-5**

When Jesus spoke of the church He did so in terms of discipline and restoration. **Matt. 18:15-17.** A humble attitude in discipline is very important. **Gal. 6:1**

e. **Elders pray for the sick**

When the sick call, elders respond. **James 5:14-15**

Praying with the sick often involves confession of sin, with accompanying counsel. The normal disciplines of silence about people's problems apply. Sin is on a need-to-know basis. Discernment is also often required. Sometimes there is a more important issue than the healing, and Elders should be sensitive to it.

f. **Elders ordain and impart gifts**

The pattern for ordination was established in the Old Testament. **Num. 27:18-25**

The New Testament both adopted and amplified the pattern. **Acts 13:1-3**

The body of Elders impart gifts and give direction. **1Tim. 1:18; 4:14; 2 Tim. 1:6**

5. **What additional comments can be made about Elders?**

   a. There is benefit in having formal theological training, but that is never made a requirement for eldership in the scriptures. All Christian elders, whether theologically trained or not, must meet the scriptural requirements for elders.

b. Some people feel that eldership is limited to males. My position is that the scriptures are weighted toward male elders, but that they do not conclusively and specifically teach that women cannot be elders. In this I distinguish between "headship" in the home and eldership in the church. I feel that this is also influenced largely by individual cultures around the world.

c. Scriptures teach that a church should have multiple elders. This saves a local church from a "one man rule." It also helps to cover each person's "blind spots."

d. The major challenge for younger churches is finding people who are qualified as elders. It is best to function under the covering of a parent church until such a time as proper elders have been developed. A church may ask "outside elders," mature believers from other churches, to serve with their own elders. This can give a church a broader perspective and make up for a lack of local elders.

e. The church has a responsibility to its elders.

They are worthy of honor.

They are worthy of double honor if they preach or teach. 1 Tim 5:17

They cannot be accused of sin unless there are several witnesses. 1 Tim 5:19

The church is to pray for and respect its leaders. Heb. 13:17-18

The church is to submit to the leadership of its elders. Heb. 13:17

HOW TO PREACH AND TEACH GOD'S WORD

The Science and Art of Preaching – 1 Tim 4:2 – Preach the WORD!

Preaching is an interaction between the preacher and the audience.

Preaching is the most visible part of the pastor's work. The science/art of preparing and delivering sermons is called homiletics in a Bible College. It is a science, because there are basic principles of communication and human nature that guide it. It is an art, because there is room for a great deal of variation and creativity in the way a sermon is presented.

1. **How can I make it clear?**

   A sermon is a speech, but also much more than a speech. It builds on the principles that govern good speech.

   Nehemiah 8:8 - There are three elements in the presentation of the Word:

   1. They made it clear. *What is God saying in this passage?*

   2. They gave meaning to the scriptures. *How can the passage be illustrated?*

   3. They helped the people understand the Word. *How can it be applied to life?*

      So you try to read clearly, and then to explain what the passage means, and finally to apply that passage to the life of the believer.

2. **Why must I consider the audience?**

   You need to know the audience to whom you are speaking.

   Evangelistic preaching is often aimed at people you may not know as well, but that means you must give special effort to learning the needs of the audience.

   Billy Graham is the world's foremost evangelist. He schedules his crusades about 2 years in advance. 6 months before the crusade starts, he begins to read the newspapers of the city he will be in. This shows him what his audience is thinking about. So when he comes to the city, he already knows what has been happening there. In his preaching, he almost always has a reference to something from that day's newspaper. And so the audience knows that he understands what their immediate concerns are.

3. **What are the elements needed in all preaching?**

   Whether you are teaching or preaching, there are several things that you should always consider:

   a. That you convey truth in your communication. – *Never be deceitful or dishonest with the Word.*

   b. That you be anointed and inspiring. – *Which comes through prayer.*

   c. That you be well prepared. – *Which comes through study.*

   d. That you present your materials in an orderly, memorable way. – *Through meditation.*

   e. That you use good principles of communication. – *Through planning.*

4. **How does the sermon look and feel?**

   Some sermons are written out word for word.

Most are preached from some kind of outline.

Some are given under the inspiration of the moment. – *There are times for each of these.*

There are also different styles of presenting the message. Most sermons are in lecture style, which is the style that most easily leads to boredom in the listener. Other styles include:

a. Drama. – *Act it out, become a character within the story.*

b. Storytelling. – *Let the story convey the truth rather than just telling the truth.*

c. Visual aids. – *Whether small or big – let it illustrate without being distractive.*

d. Question and Answer. – *Especially when teaching.*

e. Using notes.

5. What is my purpose?

A speech/sermon must have a purpose. Evangelistic sermons want people to become disciples of Christ. Sermons on tithing want people to give. Holiness sermons want people to quit sinning. But to produce action, a sermon needs certain elements.

a. You must be interesting. *If we don't awaken interest, who will pay attention?*

b. You must be clear if you are to produce action. *If you don't have a point you can't make the point.*

c. You must be convincing to produce action. There are a number of tools you use in persuading people to take action:

d. Enthusiastic suggestion.

e. Repetition.

f. Friendliness.

g. Association with people or organizations they trust.

h. Logical argument (which is the least effective tool in persuasion).

i. The goal is to produce action. – *What is it that God expects of them in the passage?*

6. What are the elements of a sermon?

A sermon has a text and a subject. Usually you preach from a single text, or perhaps a few texts that show aspects of the same truth. The subject limits you, so that you are preaching about *something*, and not *everything*. *Yet you always have a text – you are to preach the Word!*

Here is a list of things that can help you structure your

sermon:

a. **Title**. *Make it memorable*

b. **Proposition**. *Make it clear*

c. **Outline**. *Take it from the text*

d. **Notes**. *Live with the passage – take notes on life that applies to the passage*

e. **Illustrations**. *Ask yourself in preparation – how can I illustrate this point?*

f. **Exposition**. *Be completely honest with the passage – never play a one stringed guitar*

g. **Exhortation**. *What are you clearly asking the people to do as a result of this sermon?*

h. **Delivery**. *If necessary, practice – but always be aware of your technique*

7. **How do I organize the sermon?**

Once you know what you will preach about, you need to develop an *introduction* that will make people interested in hearing what you will say. *Your goal is to engage them with the passage. This could be humorous, but be careful with humor – it can easily be misunderstood. It could be a question. It could be a story.*

The *body* of the sermon will explain your idea. *Make it memorable.*

Your *conclusion* invited people to make an appropriate response. *Not always in the altar.*

8. **How do I prepare?**

You must prepare both spiritually and technically.

There is a *general preparation* that comes through regular, disciplined Bible study.

There is also a *specific preparation* for each sermon, where you carefully study the text from which you are going to preach.

Experienced preachers find that they work best when they establish a regular time in a regular, quiet, undisturbed place to study. These books or online references will be of help.

a. **A Concordance**

b. **Bible Dictionary**

c. **Commentaries**

(I am indebted to John Garlock's book, *Keys to Better Preaching*, for most of this section as well as Winston Mattsson-Boze's notes on "Preaching".)

Section 3

CONTENT
What you believe…

CONTENT – WHAT YOU BELIEVE – OUR FOUNDATIONS

To understand the basics of the Scriptures we do not have to look very far in order to find a summation of some basic, or elementary truths. In **Hebrews 5:11-6:3** the writer states emphatically that these are truths that every teacher, or for our purposes every leader, should know. The following six lessons are based on and adapted from James Beall's book, *Laying the Foundation.*

Lesson 1 - FINDING YOUR FOUNDATION

Reading - Hebrews 5:8 - 6:3

1. **What is a Foundation?**

   The term "foundation" has been borrowed from the language of building and architecture. It refers to the very first thing done in building - preparing a solid and stable support for the superstructure. The taller the building is to be, the deeper the foundation must be. Spiritually speaking, the foundation is the basis of Christian doctrine (truth) and experience - and these two are never separate - upon which all later development depends. Paul called it the "elementary teachings." **Hebrews 6:1-3**

2. **How does Christ relate to my "Foundation?"**

   Christ Himself is the only foundation that can be laid in your life, and this is done in practical experience through specific encounters with Him in obedient faith.

   a. You are built upon the foundation which is Christ by the Holy Spirit and through the ministry of those who labor with God. **1 Corinthians 3:9-11**

   b. The doctrines that become a part of your foundation were brought to you through the apostles and prophets who received the inspired Scriptures. **Ephesians 2:20**

   c. As Christ becomes your foundation through experience, you are made able to worship and find your place in His Church. **1 Peter 2:4-8, 1 Kings 5:17-18; 6:7**

3. **What are the Six Foundation Truths?**

   The writer of Hebrews lists the six basic experiences you should have with Christ before you can expect true maturity in your Christian life. These are:

   1. Repentance from dead works

   2. Faith in God

   3. Instructions about Baptisms

4. Laying on of Hands

5. Resurrection of the Dead

6. Eternal Judgment

When the writer of Hebrews tells you to leave the elementary teachings about Christ, he is literally telling you to go on from the beginning. It not only means laying the foundation, but to ground someone, to establish them, or to render firm and unwavering.

Lesson 2 - LEARNING TO TURN AROUND

Review - Hebrews 6:1-3

Reading - Psalms 51:1-19

1. What is Repentance?

Repentance is an about face from sin and acts that lead to death to the living God. It is an entire change of mind resulting in a total change of life.

a. Repentance is a command from God to all.

Acts 17:30

Repentance is not optional; it is the first response you make to Christ's Lordship. He is commanding you to turn around. Not until you have begun to turn have you acknowledged His right to rule over you.

b. Repentance is a gift from God; He enables you to repent.

Acts 5:31 - that He might give repentance

Acts 11:18 - God has granted even the Gentiles repentance unto life

2 Tim. 2:24-25 - God will grant them repentance

When God gives you the ability to repent, you suddenly realize that your actions and even your attitudes are not a private matter. You do not simply hurt yourself and other people with your sin; you offend God. This truth dawned on David as he began to see his sin as God saw it, a direct insult to His holiness and love.

c. Repentance always means turning around, changing -- turning from sin and your own ways to God. The common Bible words (O.T. Hebrew and N.T. Greek) bring out the differences in emphasis, but they overlap in the basic meaning of change.

2. How Are You Affected By The Working Of Repentance?

Repentance changes the way in your **heart** you feel about sin, about yourself as a sinner, and toward a holy but merciful God.

a. True repentance includes godly sorrow for sin.

Psalms 51:17 - a broken and contrite heart

Psalms 38:18 - KJV - I will be sorry for my sin

2 Cor. 7:8-10 - your sorrow led you to repentance

b. It includes deep humiliation as you realize your need.

Isa. 57:15 - I live with him who is contrite and lowly in spirit

c. It includes a sense of shame for evil things you have done.

Ezra 9:6 - I am too ashamed and disgraced...

d. It includes a genuine hated and loathing of sin.

Psalms 97:10 - Let those who love the Lord hate evil...

Often, when you find it difficult to be delivered from a specific habit of sin, it is because you have not yet experienced sufficient hatred for that sin.

3. **How Does The Working Of Repentance Bring About Change?**

Repentance is a complete change of mind regarding sin, a revolution in viewpoint, a revolution in your will and intellect.

a. Repentance includes recognition of sin for what it is.

Hosea 14:1-2 - forgive all our sins

b. It includes the realization that you not only do sinful things, but that you are a sinful person.

Psalms 51:5-6 - I was sinful at birth

c. It includes acknowledging that God's judgment on your sin is right and just.

Psalms 51:3-4 - you are justified when you judge

d. You accept moral responsibility for your own actions and character.

James 1:14-15 - by his own evil desire

e. You determine to do something about your sins.

Matt. 21:29 - KJV I will not, but afterward he repented, and went.

Luke 15:17-18 - I will set out and go back

f. You decide to break from sin and throw yourself on God's mercies.

Rom. 13:12-14 - put aside darkness and clothe yourself with Jesus

Lesson 3 - BECOMING FULLY PERSUADED

Review - Hebrews 6:1-3

Reading - Hebrews 11:1-6

1. How Are Repentance And Faith Related?

Repentance and faith are two sides of the same coin called justification. Repentance is the negative side of it; faith is the positive or receptive side of it. Both repentance and faith are gifts from God, initiated freely according to His grace. They are inseparable; one cannot exist without the other. It is the Holy Spirit that creates within you the response of repentance and also gives you the ability to believe.

Acts 20:21 - they must turn in repentance and have faith...

1 Thess. 1:8-9 - faith in God.. and how you turned

2. What Is Faith?

Faith is the ability to believe God: both to trust His character and to take His Word as true and reliable. Faith is your response to the persuading, convincing work of the Holy Spirit as He enables you to hear God's Word. Such persuasion results in an unshakable conviction or confidence that God's Word is true.

a. Faith is a persuasion.

Faith comes from the Greek word *pistis* (pis-tis) which means "firm persuasion; strong and welcome belief; conviction of the truth of anything."

2 Tim. 1:12 - I know whom I have believed and am convinced...

b. Faith is substance and reality.

Faith is not imagination, or the wishing of things into being. It is the conviction of truth by the inner working of the Holy Spirit, **who only persuades you to believe what actually exists.** If God gives you the faith for something, you can be sure that in the mind of God that thing really exists and is as good as yours.

Heb. 11:1 - Now faith is...

c. Faith is a gift from God

You cannot work yourself up into believing. It is not the result of mental or spiritual gymnastics. The Holy Spirit must place the ability to believe God within your heart.

Eph. 2:8 - this is not from yourselves, it is the gift of God

d. Faith is the response to hearing.

God communicates His thoughts through His Word. When He enables you to hear what He is saying to you by the Spirit, this creates within you the response of believing, of being fully persuaded that what he is saying is indeed true and directed to you.

Rom. 10:17 - faith comes from hearing the message...

4. **How Does God Persuade You To Believe?**

God uses several means today to convince you. Often it is other people or circumstances, yet the active agent of redemption in the world today is the Holy Spirit. He persuades you by His personal presence and by use of various means.

a. He uses the preaching of the Word.

1 Cor. 1:21 - through the foolishness of what was preached to save those...

b. He directly works within you to convince you of truth.

The Holy Spirit works within you to convince you that God is true and that His Word is truth. Just as He turns you from sin in repentance, He turns you to God and His Word by giving you faith.

John 16:8-11 - convicting the world

c. He will make the scriptures come alive to you.

Luke 24:32 - and opened the scriptures to us

d. His miracles are meant to help your faith.

John 10:37-38 - believe the miracles that you may know and understand...

Lesson 4 - IN THE CLOUD AND IN THE SEA

Review - Hebrews 6:1-3

Reading - 1 Cor. 10:1-2

1. **Why Does Hebrews Speak Of More Than One Baptism?**

In the text passage, Heb. 6:1-3, the word "baptisms" refers to not only the baptism in water, but also to the other baptism found in the Bible, the baptism in the Holy Spirit. These two baptisms are part of the foundation that God wants you to have in your life.

1 Cor. 10:1 - All under the cloud - all passed through the sea

1 Cor. 10:2 - Baptism in the cloud and in the sea

Baptizo = to immerse, submerge, to make overwhelmed, fully wet

a. **Baptism in the Sea - 1 Cor. 10:2**

   Ex. 14:26-30 - They went through the sea - and were baptized into Moses.

   Through this they experienced God's deliverance from the enemy.

   Mt. 3:13-17 - Jesus was baptized

   Mt. 28:18-20 - Go, make disciples, baptizing them

   Rom. 6:1-6, 11-12 - *Water Baptism Is...*

   - An outward sign... - **Col. 2:11-12** - Baptism through faith!

   - Of an inward change - **Acts 2:38** - The forgiveness of your sins

   - Crucifying your old self - **Rom. 6:6, 11** - Count Yourselves Dead

   - A resurrection to new life - **Rom. 6:4-5** - Enabling You To Serve God

b. **Baptism in the Cloud - 1 Cor. 10:2**

   Ex. 13:21-22 - The cloud was the symbol of the presence of the Lord.

   Today the Holy Spirit is the manifestation of God's presence.

   By day the cloud guided them - the Holy Spirit leads you into all truth.

   By night the cloud became a pillar of fire over them - giving them light.

   Mt. 3:11 - John said Jesus will baptize you with the Holy Spirit and with fire

   Acts 1:4-5; 8 - the Holy Spirit baptism is the fulfillment of John's statement

   Acts 2:1-4 - the Holy Spirit came with fire!

   Acts 2:38-39 - the formula - this is for all - by faith!

   Acts 8:14-17 - note vs. 12 - after belief and water baptism.

   Acts 10:44-48 - for they heard them speak with other tongues

   Acts 11:15-17 - the same gift! Received by faith.

Acts 19:1-6 - they spoke in tongues and prophesied

Lesson 5 - HANDS ARE FOR GIVING

Review - Hebrews 6:1-3

Reading - Genesis 48:8-22

1. Why Is The Hand So Important?

Throughout Scripture the hand is considered deeply significant. It is the extension of the person himself. It is his power to labor with skill and his ability to fight against enemies. God speaks of His active power in the earth as His hands. Whenever God intervened mightily in the affairs of men, they sang His praise in terms of what His hands had done.

Exodus 15:6 - Your right hand O Lord was majestic in power...

More important than all, the hand is the vehicle of blessing. You lift your hands in worship and praise to bless God. You lift your hands, extend your hands, and lay hands upon others, to communicate the blessing of God as a human channel.

2. How Were Hands Used In The Old Testament?

a. Hands were lifted in praise and worship.

   Psa. 63:4 - I will praise you... I will lift up my hands.

b. Hands were lifted in prayer.

   Psa. 141:2 - May my prayer... may the lifting up of my hands...

c. The priests communicated God's favor to the people through an uplifted, open hand.

   Lev. 9:22 - Then Aaron lifted his hands toward the people and blessed them.

d. To be consecrated actually meant to have your hands full. The Hebrew definition of the word `to consecrate' actually comes from two words; to fill, and a hand (the open one), indicating power.

   2 Chron. 29:5 - Now, who is willing to consecrate himself today to the Lord?

e. The hands were a means of transferring personal guilt to a sacrificial victim.

   i. **Lev. 1:4** - He is to lay his hand on the head...

   ii. **Lev. 4:23-24** - he is to lay his hand on the goat's head...a sin offering.

f. A superior would impart blessing to another by laying hands upon him and praying or prophesying.

    i. **Gen. 48:14-15** - Jacob blesses Joseph's sons

    ii. **Deut. 34:9** - Moses blesses Joshua

4. **How Were Hands Used In The New Testament?**

The laying on of hands was used throughout the New Testament. Jesus Himself used it as a means of giving life or virtue both in healing and in blessing. At times, the spoken word was not all He used; many times a personal touch was needed as well. Jesus' hands were a significant channel of His ministry. They should be in yours as well.

a. Hands were used to bless children.

Matt. 19:14-15 - Jesus & the children

Luke 2:25-28 - Simeon & Jesus

b. Hands were used to impart healing.

Mark 6:5 - Lay hands on a few sick people and heal them.

Mark 16:15-18 - They will lay hands on sick people and they will get well.

Acts 28:8 - placed his hands on him and healed him.

c. Hands were used to initiate people into their ministries.

Acts 6:6 - `Deacons' were set into their ministry

Acts 13:3 - They placed their hands on them and sent them off.

d. Hands were used to impart the gift of the Holy Spirit.

Acts 8:17 - Then Peter and John placed their hands on them

Acts 19:6 - When Paul placed his hands on them...

e. Hands were used to impart spiritual gifts. Webster's defines `impartation' in this way: to give or grant what one has by contact, association, or influence; to communicate or transmit.

1 Tim. 4:14 - Do not neglect your gift...

2 Tim. 1:6 - ...Fan into flame the gift of God...

Lesson 6 - WILL I STILL BE ME?

Review - Hebrews 6:1-3

Reading - 1 Cor. 15:35-50

1. **What Is Resurrection?**

Resurrection is a rising to life again after death, but it is more than that. It is also the beginning of glorification, or the changing of the physical body to share in the glorious redemption provided for the whole man by Christ. The most common Greek word for resurrection is *anastasis* (a-na-sta-sis), which simply means "to make to stand or rise up."

   a. Resurrection is the personal restoration of the individual to life.

   After the body and the soul and spirit have been separated by death - even if the body has already decomposed - God reunites these. The person's own identity is restored, including memory, recognition, the ability to communicate, etc.

   Job 19:25-27 - skin, flesh, eyes - Job expected to have this experience as a man

   b. Resurrection involves the reinfusion of life into a real corpse, resulting in the raising up to life of a literal body.

   This is not talking about reviving someone that was simply supposed to be dead and was only unconscious. This is stating that people who were unmistakably dead can experience the reversal of the processes of corruption, and by God's intervention be raised from the dead.

   Luke 24:39 - a ghost (spirit) does not have flesh and bones, as you see I have.

   c. Resurrection is the redemption of your body, God changes your body to correspond with the nature of your redeemed spirit and soul.

   While the body you receive in the resurrection will be unmistakably your own, it will not be the same frail frame that was buried. It will have been changed by the power of God and fashioned like His own.

   Phil. 3:21 - transformed lowly bodies - like his glorious body

2. **What Will Your Resurrection Body Be Like?**

The Bible provides two basic sources for information regarding you resurrection body: (1) the example of Jesus' resurrection body described in the Gospels and Acts; (2) the descriptions by analogy in Paul's letters to the Corinthians:

   a. Jesus' resurrection body was both the same and yet different from His mortal body.

      i. Jesus' resurrection body was without the limitations of His mortal body: He could appear at will, he could pass through walls, etc.

ii.   Jesus' facial appearance was sufficiently changed that His closest friends did not immediately recognize Him, but other personal characteristics identified Him as the same person.

iii. Jesus' body was not ethereal, but tangible and visible. People touched Him, saw Him, heard Him. He ate with them.

iv.   Jesus continued where He had left off in His teaching. He had remembered what His promise was and what He had and had not accomplished in the instructing of His disciples. He met them in Galilee as He had promised before His death. Evidently memory was not impaired.

3. Will Your Resurrection Body Be An Improvement On Your Present One?

Yes. God will give you a brand new body which will be far better than your present, mortal body. It will more appropriately express the spiritual treasure within.

1 Cor. 15:42-53

a.   Your new body will be imperishable - vss. 42,53

b.   Your new body will be powerful - vs. 43

c.   Your new body will be spiritual - vs. 44

d.   Your new body will be heavenly - vss. 49, 50

4. Will We Know One Another After Death And Resurrection?

This is probably the deepest question within each heart; we want to know what is going to happen to us. Will we still be the same persons we are now? Will we remember what happened to us in this life, and continue after death? Will the friendships we build in this life continue through eternity? What we are really asking is: does resurrection mean that we will continue to have personal identity? Will personality survive the grave? Thank God, the Bible gives you an emphatic "YES" in answer to these questions:

a.   Jesus Christ has always been the same person though in different bodily form.

   Heb. 13:8 - The Greek word for "same" means "one's very self, unchangeable."

   Rev. 1:18 - I am alive forevermore

b.   Job asked and answered his own question about the continuance of personality.

Job 14:14,15; 19:25-27

   c. Jesus compared resurrection life to that of the angels.

     Dan. 8:16-17 - Gabriel

   d. Paul stated that your resurrection body will have different glory from others.

     1 Cor. 15:38-42

5. **What Is The Order Of Events Of The Resurrection Of The Dead?**

   a. Firstfruits: The resurrection of Christ Himself and those who came out of their graves at the same time.

     Matt. 27:52-53 - see KJV – and came out of the graves after his resurrection...

   b. They that are Christ's at His coming.

     1 Thess. 4:16-17 - the dead in Christ will rise first

   c. Then those who are destined for destruction.

     Dan. 12:2 - multitudes ... will awake, some to everlasting life, others to shame...

     John 5:24-29 - ALL who are in their graves will hear

   d. Next, the destruction of death itself after the great white throne judgment.

     Rev. 20:11-15 - notice the progression; righteous, those in Hades, lake of fire

   e. Then the renovation of the heavens and earth, after being purged by fire.

     2 Pet. 3:10-13 - the elements will be destroyed by fire

     Rev. 21:1 - a new heaven and a new earth

6. **Will Everyone Experience Death and Resurrection?**

   This will be the norm. The Bible teaches you to prepare yourself in this life to face death, resurrection, and judgment.

   Heb. 9:27 - Just as man is destined to die once, and after that to face judgment.

   Paul emphasizes the instantaneous nature of this change.

   1 Cor. 15:51-53 - we will all be changed, in a flash

Lesson 7 - ETERNAL JUDGMENT

Review   - Hebrews 6:1-3

Reading   - John 5:17-30

1. **What Is Meant By The Term "Eternal" Judgment?**

Eternal judgment is the last of the six foundation stones to be experienced before you can really go on to maturity. As this stone is studied you will become vividly aware of the consequences of your thoughts, words, and actions. These consequences not only affect this life but also the age to come. The more real this knowledge of God's weighing your works becomes to you, the more your behavior and inner motivations are conformed to God's will through the fear of the Lord. **2 Cor. 5:9-11**

2. What Is Involved In The Process Of Judgment?

Judgment is a sorting process. God separates the good from the evil by examination, trial, and decree. The thought to remember is separation. God does not judge in the same way the earthly courts do, by examining the evidence, hearing arguments on both sides, and then rendering a verdict. God has no need to ascertain guilt or merit because He already knows all things.

Heb. 4:13 Pro. 15:11

3. Will There Be Degrees Of Reward And Punishment?

The basis for all judgment is the gospel of Jesus Christ.

Rom. 2:16   John 3:16-21

Knowledge of God and of His gospel is not equally available to all peoples in the world. When God judges He will take into account the amount of light you had and what you did with it.

a. Those who are not believers will be judged according to the law written on their hearts and in their conscience. **Rom. 2:12-16**

b. Christians will be judged according to the gospel. Also they will be held accountable for the amount of revelation they received of God's will and provisions for them. More light means more responsibility.

Luke 12:47-48   John 9:39-41

c. Christian leaders will be judged more severely than other believers. They will be held accountable not only for their own lives but for the souls of those committed to their care.

James 3:1   Heb. 13:17   Mat. 18:5-6

d. Those that hear the gospel but reject it will be judged more severely than those who never heard. **John 12:47-48   John 15:22**

4. What Opportunities Are There For Self-Judgment?

a. Communion provides a regular discipline of self-examination. - **1 Cor. 11:28**

b. God uses tests and trials of faith to help you discover your reactions under pressure.

James 1:2-4   **Rom. 5:3-5**

c. The ministry of the Holy Spirit within you causes you to know your own heart.

1 Sam. 10:6   **2 Cor. 3:18**

d. The Lord uses spiritual leadership to help you recognize your faults and errors.

Heb. 13:17   **Titus 3:10-11**

e. God may use times of affliction to call your attention to an area of sin in your life.

James 5:14-16

5. **What Is The Purpose Of The Great White Throne Judgment?**

The Great White Throne Judgment is the scene of the final examination for all people. The purpose of judging is not to determine guilt or innocence. Nor is it to decide everyone's future destiny. These are already known. But this judgment will demonstrate the necessity of God's decision of condemnation or commendation. God will bring to light every secret thought and motivation as well as every deed. Each person will see in the light of God's perfection why his deeds were either evil or righteous. His own conscience will agree with the judgment he receives from the Lord. The books will be opened to the record of everyone's ways and works.

Rev. 20:11-15   **Jer. 17:10**

a. Justice is completed at the Great White Throne. - **Rom. 2:5-10**

b. Works will be eternally rewarded.   **Gal. 6:7-10**

6. **How Should This Knowledge Of Eternal Judgment Affect You Now?**

Knowledge of eternal judgment is not merely head knowledge; it should change your behavior.

God has put a lot of information in the Bible regarding the future for a reason: He is seeking to influence your motivation.

Rom. 11:22   **2 Cor. 5:11**

CONTENT – WHAT YOU BELIEVE – OUR SALVATION

The following notes have been compiled in an outline form and can be used to assist in the study of the topic of Our Salvation. It would be most helpful if you have your Bible open to 1 Peter as you read these notes. **The text in 1 Peter** will help you understand these notes that are meant to explain and expound on the topics introduced in the text.

Introduction

According to the Wycliffe Bible Encyclopedia the name given to the study of the doctrine of salvation is *soteriology*. Wycliffe defines this as, "the doctrine of salvation as revealed in the Bible and formulated by an inductive study of the Scriptures". While an inductive study will certainly give the student a general knowledge of what *our salvation* is all about, none other than the Apostle Peter has already done much of this work. In the first two chapters of his first epistle he gives a detailed description of *our salvation*. But, before looking at Peter's statements, let's look at both Paul and John's thoughts about *our salvation*.

Romans 10:8-17–To Paul, *our salvation* is based on confession, belief and faith.

vs. 9 – *saved = to save, i.e. deliver or protect (literally or figuratively)*

vs. 10 – *salvation = rescue or safety (physically or morally)*

Rev. 12:10 – To John, *our salvation* is a present reality.

salvation = soteria – see above

1. Our Election   1 Peter 1:1-2

1:1

NIV - To God's elect, strangers in the world, scattered throughout…

NKJ – …to the pilgrims of the Dispersion…

Heb. 11:13-16 – We are pilgrims here on earth!

The districts mentioned by Peter all lie in the northeast corner of Asia Minor, where Paul was forbidden to evangelize in Acts 16:6-10. Also notice the circular nature of the districts listed, and that the recipients were mainly Gentiles. Peter takes a term uniquely Jewish, and applies it to both Jewish and Gentile Christians.

1:2

⇒ *chosen according to foreknowledge* - **Rom. 8:28-30; Eph. 1:7-11**

⇒ *sanctifying* - to make holy, purify, or consecrate – **2 Thes. 2:13**

⇒ *sprinkling by his blood* - Mentioned in the O.T. in regards to 4 occasions.

   a. **Lev. 14:1-7** – the priest would sprinkle a person cleansed from skin diseases

   b. **Ex. 29:20-21** – when Moses consecrated Aaron and his sons

   c. **Ex. 24:1-8** – when Moses sprinkled the people as they ratified the covenant

   d. **Ex. 12 & Heb. 11:28** – when the blood was sprinkled at the Passover celebration

2. Our Hope   1 Peter 1:3-4

__1:3__

⇒ *new birth* - **Jn. 3:1-8; Acts 2:37-39; Rom. 3:23;5:8;6:23;10:9-10**.

__1:3__

⇒ *hope* - expectation, confidence or pleasurable anticipation **Rom. 5:3-4**

⇒ *resurrection* - **1 Cor. 15:12-20**.

He was...so you will! **1 Cor. 15:42-44** – your resurrection body will be incorruptible, glorious, powerful, spiritual and eternal

__1:4__

⇒ *inheritance* - Old Testament – physical   New Testament - spiritual

⇒ *perish* - The 'land' was taken from natural Israel and fell into decay. Your inheritance in the Spirit will never perish, spoil or fade.

⇒ *kept* - reserved - the verb signifies *keeping* as the result of *guarding*.

3. Our Trials   1 Peter 1:5-9

__1:5__

⇒ *through faith* - **Heb. 11:6**

⇒ *shielded* - A military term - to post a guard; to hem in or protect." **Phil. 4:6-8** – Keeping your mind shielded is a cooperative effort.

⇒ *coming... salvation* - **Rom. 13:11**

⇒ *revealed* - last day judgment **1 Pet. 1:13, 4:13; 2 Thess.**

1:6-7; 1 Cor. 1:7

1:6

⇒ *rejoice* – a deep spiritual joy - also in 1:8 - **Lk. 1:46-47; Acts 16:34**

⇒ *though now* - These believers are rejoicing *even though* they may suffer grief.

1:7

⇒ *your faith... as gold* – **Jer. 6:27-30; Psa. 66:10-12; 2 Chron. 32:31**

⇒ *praise, glory and honor* - **Rom. 2:29; 1 Cor. 4:5**

1:8

⇒ *seen* - to see with the eyes *see* - to discern clearly, fully comprehend

⇒ *believe* - to trust or rest one's confidence in, or to depend upon.

⇒ *joy* - to leap for joy, spin about

1:9

⇒ *receiving* - You are receiving, now in part, what you will always be receiving.

4. Our Realization   1 Peter 1:10-12

1:10-12

The O.T. prophets did not really understand their own revelations of God's plan. Prophets, Kings and Angels have all desired to look into what is now realized in your life – *our salvation.*

Lk. 10:24

⇒ *to look into* - to stoop sideways... one stooping and stretching the neck to gaze upon some wonderful sight.
Jn. 20:5

5. Our Holiness   1 Peter 1:13-21

1:13

The balance of Peter's thoughts deal with the practical aspects of applying in everyday life this 'salvation of your souls' (vs. 9).

⇒ *prepare your minds* - be ready for the most strenuous mental endeavor.

⇒ *be self-controlled* - be sober - this phrase has two meanings - 1- to refrain from drunkenness 2- be steady in their minds

⇒ *set your hope* - Christians who live in hope can endure the trials of the present.

1:14

⇒ *As obedient children* - obedience should be their mother **2 Cor. 2:9**

    1- Parents - Eph. 6:1-2

    2- Leaders - Heb. 13:17

    3- Civil - Rom. 13:1-7

⇒ *do not conform* - conforming to something that changes and so is illusory

1:15-16

⇒ *holy* - In the Greek language this word has three parts to its definition.

    1- physically pure

    2- morally blameless

    3- spiritually consecrated

⇒ *in all you do* - general behavior, life style – **2 Cor. 6:14 – 7:1**

1:17

⇒ *judges*   - The Father judges - **Rom. 2:1-4**

               - He ONE DAY will - **Rom. 2:5-11**

⇒ *each man's work* - The judgment of God is based on the works of man.

2 Chron. 6:23; Psa. 62:12; Jer. 17:9-10; Mat. 16:27; 1 Cor. 3:12-15; 2 Cor. 5:7-10; Rev. 20:11-15; Rev. 22:12

⇒ *impartially* - This is the earliest known Christian word not found outside of Christian writings. **Acts 10:34; Rom. 2:11; Jms. 2:1**

⇒ *live your lives as strangers* - Your home is heaven and the *city of God.*

Heb. 11:8-10,13-16

⇒ *in reverent fear* - This fear is based on the fact of the coming judgment of God.

1:18

⇒ *perishable things* – Jesus' blood can purchase redemption, and will not perish.

⇒ *redeemed* - a ransom-price - **Luke 24:21; Titus 2:14**

    a. To repurchase a forfeited inheritance - Yours. **Lev.**

25:23-28

    b. To ransom a relative from a foreigner - Satan. **Lev. 25:47-49**

    c. None for the intentional murderer - Satan. **Num. 35:19, 31**

1:19

⇒ *a lamb* - referring to the Passover Lamb. **Ex. 12:5; Isa. 53:7.** John the Baptist also applied this term to Jesus. **Jn. 1:29, 36**

1:20

⇒ *chosen before* - The plan for your redemption was not devised in an emergency.

1:21

⇒ *believe* - The basis for your salvation - **Rom. 10:9-10**

⇒ *faith and hope* - These must rest in God - there is no other. **Rom. 5:1-5**

6. Our Love 1 Peter 1:22-25

1:22

⇒ *purified* - described the purification of the people and priests

⇒ *love for your brothers* - philadelphia = brotherly love

⇒ *sincere* – unfeigned - from two Greek words; 'not' and 'actor'

⇒ *love one another* - agapao = sacrificial, a determination of the will.

⇒ *deeply* - using supreme effort, with every muscle strained - **Rom. 5:8**

1:23

⇒ *born again* - **Jn. 3:1-8**

⇒ *of incorruptible seed* - The seed itself (of your salvation) is the Holy Spirit.

⇒ *living and enduring* - **2 Tim. 3:16-17; Heb. 4:12**

1:24

⇒ *like grass* – wild grass that grows for a bit and then is gone. **Mat. 6:30; 14:19; Isa. 40:6-8**

1:25

⇒ *the word* - What can give hope of permanence? *The word of the Lord!*

7. Our Growth   1 Peter 2:1-3

2:1

⇒ *rid yourselves* - laying aside, a stripping off of one's clothes. **Ezk. 18:31-32; Rom. 13:12; Eph. 4:22-25; Col. 3:5-10; Heb. 12:1; Jms. 1:21**

⇒ *malice* - badness in quality, as in the opposite of excellence

⇒ *deceit* - to decoy, to use trickery

⇒ *hypocrisy* – (1:22) consistently acting a part and concealing real motives

⇒ *envy* - all ill-will or jealousy.

⇒ *slander* - speaking against someone or gossiping which takes place when the victim is not there to defend themselves.

2:2-3

⇒ *crave*- This command is based on the assumption that you will obey vs. 1. It is the positive command in contrast to the negative command in vs. 1.

⇒ *pure* - sincere - a term that describes corn that is entirely free from chaff, dust or useless, harmful matter. **Ps. 19:7-10; Heb. 5:12-13**

⇒ *tasted* - **Ps. 34:8**.

8. Our Sacrifices   1 Peter 2:4-10

2:4-5

⇒ *the living Stone* - **Isa. 28:16**.

⇒ *rejected* - disallowed - to disapprove **Mk. 8:31; Lk. 20:9-19**

⇒ *chosen* - select, by implication, favorite. - As you receive Him you become a 'favorite' one - **1 Pet. 2:4,6, 9; Mt. 22:14; Rev. 17:14**

⇒ *precious* – valued - **1 Pet. 1:19**

⇒ *living stones* - **1 Ki. 5:17-18; 6:7; Eph. 2:20-22**

⇒ *are being built* - a house-builder, to construct **Eph. 2:21-22;4:15-16**

⇒ *holy priesthood* - Jesus is the High Priest, believers are a holy priesthood

⇒ *spiritual sacrifices* -

    1) Your life – Rom. 12:1

    2) Your loot – Phil. 4:15-19

3) Your lips – Heb. 13:15

2:6

⇒ *cornerstone* - **Isa. 28:16; Rom. 9:33**

2:7

⇒ *this stone* - **Psa. 118:22-23; Mark 12:10; Acts 4:11**

2:8

⇒ *to stumble… fall* - **Isa. 8:14-15; Mt. 21:42-44**

⇒ *destined for* - **Rom. 9:14-24**

2:9

Peter now applies to the Church all these Old Testament names for the people of God. The Church includes the people of faith in every generation… YOU!

⇒ *chosen people* - **Ex. 19:5-6; Dt. 7:6; 14:2**

⇒ *royal priesthood* - Christians are both royalty and priestly through Christ.

⇒ *holy nation* - **Isa. 62:12**

⇒ *special people* – that's you

2:10

⇒ *Once… but now* - **Hosea 1:6, 9-10; 2:23**

9. **Our Works   1Peter 2:11-12**

2:11

⇒ *aliens and strangers* - **Gen. 23:4; Ps. 39:12**

⇒ *abstain* - **Acts 15:20,29;1 Tim. 4:3**

⇒ *sinful desires* = unbridled impulses - **Rom. 1:24; 6:12; Gal. 5:16**

⇒ *war against your soul* - **Jms. 1:13-15; 4:1-2**

2:12

⇒ *live such good lives* - conversation - see notes on 1:15-16

⇒ *good* - the coming theme - **2:15-16, 20; 3:1-2; Tit. 3:4-8; Eph. 2:8-10**

⇒ *visits us* = observing or inspecting, or the day of looking upon. **2 Cor. 5:10; Heb. 9:27**

CONTENT – WHAT YOU BELIEVE – OUR HISTORY

RESTORATION OF TRUTH AS SEEN IN THE CHURCH - THEN AND NOW

INTRODUCTION - A Look at the Big Picture

The Church began with a handful of seeming misfits and reluctant followers in an obscure region of the world known as Judaea. Since that time Christianity has grown to become the faith of nearly one-third of the earth's population. It has spread at a phenomenal rate and has become more deeply rooted in more lives and more cultures than any other religion in the history of mankind. In addition the Christian community has experienced a growth in maturity which matches the outward expansion in numbers and prestige.

The Church's strength is even all the more remarkable when you consider not only the competition from other religions and philosophies, but even the downright persecution and severe opposition to the faith throughout all of history. From the attacks of Celsus and Lucian of Samosata in the second century, to those of Voltaire in the eighteenth and Karl Marx in the nineteenth, and the outright hostility of H.L. Mencken, Adolph Hitler and the Communist Leaders of China in the twentieth century, Christianity has not only held its own but continued to expand.

The early history of Christianity is unique since it laid the foundation for all later expressions of the Christian faith. What the apostles taught and practiced became the true pattern for all later teaching and practice, and the standard by which they would be judged.

Church History, then, can be viewed through the prism of truth. The Church began when Truth was revealed. History continues into the dark ages as Truth is rejected. Then Truth is restored during the reformation.

Peter foretold this concept in Acts 3:19-21.

*19 Repent, then, and turn to God, so that your sins may be wiped out, that **times of refreshing** may come from the Lord, 20 and that he may send the Christ, who has been appointed for you — even Jesus. 21 **He must remain in heaven until the time comes for God to restore everything**, as he promised long ago through his holy prophets. NIV*

Jesus is being held in heaven, He is remaining in heaven, and He is not returning a second time – until the time comes for God to restore everything. What began in 1517, the restoration of truth, or the first of many "times of refreshing," will continue until

Jesus' second coming! This is our paradigm for understanding the restoration of truth. Truth was revealed through the first coming of Jesus. Truth was historically rejected by the world. And then God has been restoring truth as He prepares the world for Jesus' second coming.

THE MAIN PERIODS OF CHURCH HISTORY

TRUTH REVEALED - Early Church - Christ to 140 AD

1. **The Early Church recognized that Jesus is the Truth**

   John 18:38 - Pilate's eternal question – What is truth?

   John 14:6 - Jesus' eternal_answer – I am the truth!

   Matthew Henry's Commentary states;

   "Jesus is the truth; as truth is opposed to figure and shadow Heb. 9:24, Jn. 6:32, Heb. 8:2, as truth is opposed to falsehood and error; the doctrine of Christ is true doctrine, and as truth is opposed to_fallacy and deceit; he is true to all that trust in him, as true as truth itself, 2 Cor. 1:20."

   Barne's Notes (Commentary) states;

   "Jesus is the source of truth, or he who originates and communicates truth for the salvation of men. Truth is a representation of things as they are. The life, the purity, and the teaching of Jesus Christ was the most complete and perfect representation of the things of the eternal world that has been or can be presented to man. The ceremonies of the Jews were shadows; the life of Jesus was the truth. The opinions of men are fancy, but the doctrines of Jesus were nothing more than a representation of facts as they exist in the government of God. **Col. 2:16-17"**

2. **The Early Church had Truth**

   1 Peter 1:3-4 – everything we need for life and godliness

   1 Peter 1:19 – we have the word of the prophets made more certain

   Eph. 3:3-5 – it has now been revealed by the Spirit

   - Salvation by faith and repentance- Acts 16:30-31 (Heb. 6:1-2)

   - Water baptism by immersion - Acts 8:38-39

   - Holy Spirit baptism - Acts 2:4

   - Laying on of hands with prophecy - Acts 13:3

   - Resurrection of the dead - 1 Cor. 15:20,52

   - Eternal judgment - 1 Cor. 11:31-32, Rev. 20:

11-15

- Holiness of spirit, soul and body - 1 Peter 1: 13-16

- Healing of physical bodies - Acts 5:16

- Deliverance from evil spirits - Acts 16:18

- Gifts of the Spirit - 1 Cor. 12:7-11

- Fruits of the Spirit - Gal. 5:22-23

- Ascension gift ministries - Eph. 4:11

- Spiritual worship - John 4:23-24

- Sacraments (marriage, communion...) - 1 Cor. 7:11; 11:23-28

- Church discipline - 1 Cor. 5:12-13

3. Why Christianity Expanded – 33 – 140 AD

Eerdmans' Handbook to the History of Christianity states,

"Several factors encouraged the rapid spread of Christianity. One was the existence of a unifying language and culture, at least in the cities, from Italy to India. In the east Alexander the Great and his successors established Greek as the common language - often referred to as *koine,* the Greek word for 'common'. Paul and other early Christians were able to use this language to spread their message.

Jews were scattered throughout the Empire and beyond and provided Christian missionaries with an entry into the pagan world. Since the first Christians were Jews, they used the synagogues, both inside and outside Judea, as ready-made centers for evangelism. (The Jews mandated that whenever there were 10 family heads living on one location then a synagogue had to be built.)

Three hundred years of peace and general prosperity prevailed throughout the Roman Empire from the time of Augustus, with a few notable exceptions. This has become known as the *pax Romana* (Roman peace). It allowed great freedom of travel throughout the Mediterranean world. For example, Paul could travel along superbly engineered roads, and also expect the protection of the Roman government (because of his Roman citizenship) until the final years of his life."

4. Rome versus Christ

In the beginning of the Church the Roman authorities treated Christianity as a sect of Judaism, protected under

Roman law. As soon as it became apparent that there was a difference, then persecution began.

The *Christian History* magazine published the following information.

"From its fledgling years as a despised and illicit religious sect, Christianity endured some three centuries of violence and hostility to emerge as the dominant force in the Roman Empire and as a faith that continues to shape the world.

Persecution in the Roman Empire was not, as is widely supposed, a constant experience for Christians. Rather, it was sporadic, spaced sometimes by long periods of relative tranquility. Neither was persecution always Empire wide; more often, particularly in the first two centuries, it was localized. Inflamed rumors, perhaps based on the early Christian's observance of the Eucharist and love feasts, accused believers of cannibalism and incest.

Many Christians 'lapsed' (a term used for those who compromised their faith by complying with imperial directives or cooperating with government authorities) under the threat of persecution. The numbers of those who fell away produced a crisis for the church in the 250s. Eventually the question of whether to readmit the lapsed produced several splits. The church allowed flight in order to escape persecution and warned against rushing into a voluntary martyrdom.

The high regard for the martyrs as the heroes of the church and the privileges assigned to them led to the cult of the saints.

Perhaps the most severe persecution, the 'Great Persecution,' initiated by Emperor Diocletian, was also the last, beginning in 303 and continuing off and on in places until 324.

It is estimated that more people have been martyred for Christ in the past 50 years than in the church's first 300 years."

a. **Nero - 64**

It is generally recognized that Nero spearheaded the first persecutions backed_by the Roman government.

A Roman historian, Tacitus, gave us the details of Nero's actions. After setting fire to Rome Nero tried to shift the blame on to Christians. Tacitus wrote, "First those who confessed to being

Christians were arrested. Then, on information obtained from them, hundreds were convicted, more for their anti-social beliefs than for fire-raising. In their deaths they were made a mockery. They were covered in the skins of wild animals, torn to death by dogs, crucified or set on fire - so that when darkness fell they burned like torches in the night." This ultimately aroused the sympathy of the populace against Nero.

Sometimes the length and severity of these persecutions seem to be exaggerated, but the Book of Revelation does verify that what began under Nero continued through to the time that Emperor Domitian (81-96 AD) reigned.

Surviving letters prove that by 111 AD profession of Christianity could be a capital offense.

b. Ignatius - 110-115

Ignatius was the bishop of the church at Antioch early in the second century. What little is known of him comes almost entirely from 7 letters written during his journey to Rome to be executed, sometime between 110-115 AD.

History reveals that Ignatius possessed the gift of prophecy, although he personally considered himself inferior to the apostles. He was so enthusiastic about becoming a martyr that he begged the Christians in Rome not to prevent his expected execution.

His seven letters were addressed to churches and to Polycarp, the bishop of Smyrna. In them he argued passionately about several doctrinal stands. He believed that there should be one bishop in charge of each congregation in order to prevent splits and to ensure that pure doctrine was preserved. He also condemned the Docetist ideas current in churches in Asia Minor, where it was held that Jesus only seemed to be a man, and was in fact a pure spirit-being, uncontaminated by this material world.

Ignatius thought of his own journey to Rome for execution as a conscious imitation of the Lord's last journey to Jerusalem and the cross. During this time martyrdom became regarded by many as the ultimate sign of Christian discipleship.

c. Polycarp - 156-160

Polycarp, the bishop of Smyrna (Izmir in modern Turkey), became a martyr when he was around 86 between the years of 156-160 AD. One of Polycarp's disciples, Eusebius, so elevated Polycarp's execution that people started to venerate his death on an annual basis. This celebration became the pattern for the practice of venerating a martyr's remains and commemorateing their death. Later the belief developed that prayers addressed to God through the martyrs were especially effective.

In the late 200s and early 300s the practice of the veneration of the martyr's grew rapidly. The events of the last and violent persecutions led to an exaggeration of the scale and extent of earlier persecutions. The numbers of martyrs and their sufferings were greatly magnified; the stories of their deaths were embroidered with all sorts of fantastic miraculous happenings and superstitions. Some converts from paganism brought with them pre-Christian ideas so that in the church the martyrs began to take on the role that the gods had earlier played in the old religions.

d. Justin Martyr - 165

Justin's pupil Tatian referred to him as "the most admirable Justin." Tertullian spoke of him as a "philosopher and martyr." Hippolytus called him simply "the martyr." Almost all scholars agree that Justin is one of the greatest of the early defenders of the faith, or apologists. Before his unusual conversion he had studied one after the other of the current philosophical systems - Stoicism, Aristotelianism, Pythagoreanism and Platonism. The one day, as he describes it, he stood near the Aegean Sea just outside the city of Ephesus and an old man approached him.

"Does philosophy produce happiness?" asked the old man.

"Absolutely," Justin replied, "and it alone."

Then in an extended conversation the old man suggested to Justin that there were many questions Plato could not answer, but there is a true philosophy with an explanation for all questions. That philosophy is Christianity. After a lengthy discussion the old man walked on, never to be seen again by Justin. Justin says of that encounter; "I never saw him again, but my spirit was immediately set on fire, and affection for the prophets, and for those who are friends of Christ, took hold of me; while pondering his words, I discovered that his was the only true and useful philosophy. Thus is it that I am now a [true] philosopher."

Classical Readings in Christian Apologetics by L. Russ Bush states the following.

"After his conversion Justin became a professor of philosophical Christianity in his own private school in Rome. Since he was a layman, he probably operated the school in his home. He also seems to have traveled considerably throughout the Roman Empire, spending his time in a ministry of teaching and evangelism.

In the year 167 AD Justin and six others were brought to trial, charged with the crime of being Christians. All of them admitted to the charge. They were scourged and then beheaded."

Justin was one of the most notable 'apologists' of the entire second century. His three surviving books are *First Apology, Second Apology,* and his longest *Dialogue with Trypho.*

TRUTH REJECTED - 140 – 1517 AD

1. The Decline of Truth - 140 - 324 AD

a. Tolerance of Heresies

(1) Gnostics

Gnosticism probably has its roots in Acts 8, with the life of Simon Magus the Sorcerer. According to Eerdmans' *Handbook of the History of Christianity,* the Gnostics were followers of a variety of religious movements which stressed that people could be saved through a secret knowledge (*gnosis* in Greek). This movement became more formalized in the second century. In Gnostic belief they set a transcendent God over against an ignorant creator (who is often a caricature of the God of the Old Testament). All Gnostics viewed the material creation as evil. Sparks of divinity, however, have been encapsulated in the bodies of certain 'spiritual' individuals destined for salvation. These 'spirituals' are ignorant of their heavenly origins. God sends down to them a redeemer who brings them salvation in the form of 'secret knowledge' of themselves, their origin and their destiny. Thus awakened, the 'spirituals' escape from the prison of their bodies at death and pass safely through the planetary regions controlled by hostile demons, to be reunited with God. Since salvation depended solely on the knowledge of one's 'spiritual' nature then it mattered not at all how one lived - which lead to a very licentious lifestyle - as they claimed that they were 'pearls' who could not be stained by any external mud. The most famous Gnostic teacher was *Valentinus*, who taught at Alexandria and who came to Rome in 140 AD. He had a number of able followers, among them *Theodotus* in the East, and *Ptolemy* and *Heracleon* in the West. *Heracleron's* commentary on the Gospel of John is the earliest known commentary on a New Testament book.

(2) Marcionites

Marcion arrived in Rome in 140 AD and immediately fell under the spell of the Gnostic teacher, *Cerdo*, who believed that the God of the Old Testament was different from the God and Father of the Lord Jesus Christ. The God of the Old Testament was unknowable; the latter had been revealed. The former was sheer justice; whereas the God of the New Testament is loving and gracious. *Marcion* stated that Jesus Christ was not born of a woman; he suddenly appeared in the synagogue at Capernaum in 29 AD as a grown man. Jesus was not like any other human, he was a new being on earth. Christ's human experiences and sufferings were merely apparent, not real. Since creation was not an act of the good God of the New Testament, the Christian must reject the world. The body must be denied and discarded, since the soul and spirit alone are redeemed. As a result Marcion rejected the doctrine of the resurrection of the body. The Marcionites set up their own churches, modeled on orthodox congregations. They had their own orders of clergy and rituals, but declined in influence as they linked with the Manichaeans.

(3) Montanists

An enthusiastic young Christian named Montanus began to attract attention as a prophet in 172 AD in Phrygia, a region of western Asia Minor. Two prophetesses, Prisca and Maximilla, soon joined him. They claimed to be mouthpieces of the Paraclete, the Greek title for the Holy Spirit. At times God spoke through them in first person. They were the 'New Prophecy". Through their oracles they urged Christians to relish persecution: "Do not hope to die in bed … but as martyrs." Montanists were 'gloriously martyred' in Gaul and Africa. Montanists called on Christians to a demanding asceticism. Marital relations were to be abandoned in favor of chastity, fasts multiplied, and food eaten dry. They were known for their gifts of the Spirit, their visions, speaking in tongues and their intense religious excitement. Maximilla once predicted: "After me there will be no prophecy, but the End!" Her predictions were not fulfilled. Their prophecies also contradicted what was becoming known as the accepted canon of scripture. Despite their excesses, the Montanists stood for the conviction that the Spirit was as active in the contemporary Church as He was at the beginning; greater manifestations, not lesser, were promised for the 'last days'. In reacting to them, the mainstream Church lost much of its zeal and enthusiasm, as it were, throwing out the baby with the bath water.

(4) Neo-Platonism

According to Williston Walker in *A History of the Christian Church*, Neo-Platonism was founded in Alexandria by Ammonius Saccas in 245 AD, while its real developer was Platonius who had settled in Rome in 244 AD. This religion was a pantheistic, mystical interpretation of Plato's philosophies. God is simple, absolute existence, all perfect, from whom the lower existences come. He is the One from whom the 'world-soul' derives its being, and from that individual souls. From the 'world-soul' the realm of matter comes. Their morals were ascetic, and their conception of salvation was that of a rising of the soul to God in mystic contemplation, the end of which was union with the divine. This philosophy strongly influenced such men as Augustine.

(5) Manichaeans

Mani was born in Persia in 216 AD and began preaching his philosophy in Babylon in 242 AD where he was martyred in 277 AD. Mani's goal was to establish the final world religion and community. He incorporated elements of Zoroastrianism, Buddhism, Judaism, and Christianity, recognizing each as a step that prepared you for the universal message he proclaimed. Light and darkness, good and evil are essentially at war. Salvation was based on Gnosticism in that right knowledge of man's true nature, and a desire to return to the realm of light, coupled with the rejection of all that pertained to darkness - especially physical appetites and desires - would bring one to God. This movement absorbed the remnants of the Christian-Gnostic sects and other heresies. Before his conversion, Augustine was an adherent of this heresy. Manichaeism's influence was felt until the later part of the 1300s.

b. Tolerance of Sinful Lifestyles

(1) Compromise

As is still true today, doctrine and lifestyle go hand in hand. When the Church started to compromise truth then their lifestyles became less holy. In the late 200s came the first deliberate attempts by Christian missionaries to 'baptize' features of pagan religions, and thus overcoming them by absorbing them into Christianity. Churches took over the temples, martyrs replaced the old gods in popular devotion, and the festivals of the Christian year took the place of the high-days and holy days of paganism. In Armenia the conversion of the royal family brought about the acceptance of Christianity as their new national religion, whether repentance was there or not. Superficial methods of evangelism became common throughout Europe, with a victory-whatever-the-cost mentality setting in.

(2) Conformity

As Christianity spread there was tremendous pressure to conform to worldly influences. How far this went can be seen in a single illustration. The Council of Elvira, now Granada in Spain in 313 AD provided that Christians who as magistrates wore the garments of a pagan priesthood could be restored after 2 years of penance, provided they had not actually sacrificed or paid for the sacrifice.

c. 'Victory' over Persecution

(1) Diocletian

91

In 284 AD Diocletian became the Roman Emperor. He was a man who had great abilities as a civil administrator and he was determined to reorganize the empire so as to provide more adequate military defense, prevent army conspiracies aiming at a change of Emperors, and render the internal administration more efficient. He initiated sweeping reforms that rendered the senators powerless, and the Emperor all-powerful. He abandoned Rome and made Nicomedia in Asia Minor his capital. To such a power hungry man the Church presented a serious threat. It must have seemed a state within the state over which he had no control. The Church was rapidly growing in numbers and strength. Two courses lay open for a ruler, either to force it into submission and break its power, or to enter into alliance with it and thus secure political control of the growing organism. The latter was to be the method of Constantine, the former the attempt of Diocletian. Diocletian sub-divided the East to Galerius, who was even more hostile to Christianity, and had much influence over Diocletian. Diocletian first purged the army of all Christians and then began a rapid succession of edicts. In February, 303 AD, by three great edicts Churches were ordered destroyed, sacred books confiscated, clergy imprisoned and forced to sacrifice by torture. In 304 AD a fourth edict required all Christians to offer sacrifices. It was a time of fearful persecution, with many martyrs and many more who 'lapsed'. When Diocletian voluntarily retired in 305 AD the persecution stopped on an empire-wide scale, although pockets continued to exist and actually escalate in the East under Galerius. An edict of toleration was issued in 311 AD "on condition that nothing is done by them (Christians) contrary to discipline."

(2) Constantine

After the death of Galerius in May, 311 AD, there began a struggle to gain control of the Empire. Constantine, a ruler in the East, had inadequate forces for his fight against the Western ruler, Maxentius. It is unclear if Constantine considered himself a Christian at this time. As the battle approached in an area a little to the north of Rome, Constantine had a dream. He saw the initial letters of the name of Christ with the words, "By this sign you will conquer." Taking this as an omen, he had the monogram hastily painted on his helmet and on the shields of his soldiers, and so in some sense he entered the conflict as a Christian. On October 28, 312, occurred one of the decisive struggles of history, in which Maxentus lost the battle and his life. The West was Constantine's! The Christian God, he believed, had given him the victory, and every Christian impulse was confirmed. He was, thenceforth, in all practical aspects a Christian, even though pagan emblems still appeared on coins, and he retained the title of Pontifex Maximus. In 313 Constantine permitted full freedom to Christianity in what has generally become known as the Edict of Milan. It proclaimed absolute freedom of conscience, placed Christianity on a full legal equality with any religion of the Roman world, and ordered the restoration of all Church property confiscated in the previous persecutions. A seeming great victory for the Church had taken place. But in winning its freedom from its enemies, it had come largely under the control of the ruler of the Roman imperial throne. A fateful union with the state had begun.

2. The Continued Decline of Truth - 324 - 590

a. All are commanded to become Christians

(1) Constantine and the Church - 311-337

In the *Handbook to the History of Christianity* (Eerdmans') it states that the main question being asked in the 300's was the question asked by Bishop Donatus when presented with an unfavorable decree from emperor Constans, "What has the Emperor to do with the Church?" From the very beginning of Constantine's reign, most Christians agreed with the Emperor that he had a great deal to do with the Church. Although they later complained about the Emperor's interference, it was the Donatists who first asked Constantine to intervene, less than 6 months after he assumed control of the Empire. The Donatists were a strict party in North Africa who refused to recognize Caecilian as bishop of Carthage because, they alleged, he had been ordained by a *traditor*, one who had 'handed over' or 'betrayed' Scriptures to the authorities in the recent persecution.

The Roman Emperor, as head of the state religion, had always been responsible for maintaining good relations between the people and their gods. Constantine naturally saw himself in a similar role as Christian Emperor. Why the Church asked for and accepted his intervention is curious. Part of the reason was purely selfish, one faction wanting clout against the other. But it could also be that the Church desired a return to an Old Testament pattern, where the King was supposed to promote all things pertaining to the Mosaic Law.

When Constantine became master of the East in 324, he found a dispute already raging between Alexander, bishop of Alexandria, and one of his presbyters, Arius. Arius was attempting to solve the difficult problem of the relation of the Son to God the Father. He suggested that the Son, though Creator, was himself created and therefore could not be truly divine like the Father. Alexander and his bishops judged this heretical and excommunicated Arius, who found support elsewhere in the East. Constantine hoped to settle the matter 'out of court' and sent a letter to the contending parties describing the dispute as 'very trifling and indeed unworthy to be the cause of such a conflict. When he saw the dispute was not to be settled so easily Constantine called a council of the whole Church, the first general council, at Nicaea in 325. The Emperor himself presided over the critical session, and it was he who proposed the reconciling word, *homoousios*, or of one essence, to describe Christ's relationship to the Father. All but Arius and 2 other bishops accepted this compromise.

Constantine founded Constantinople in 330 and thus shifted the focus of the Empire eastward, contributing both to the decline of the West and the independence of the Western Church.

(2) The Edict of Milan - 313

When I, Constantine Augustus, as well as I Licinius Augustus d fortunately met near Mediolanurn (Milan), and were considering everything that pertained to the public welfare and security, we thought -, among other things which we saw would be for the good of many, those regulations pertaining to the reverence of the Divinity ought certainly to be made first, so that we might grant to the Christians and others full authority to observe that religion which each preferred; whence any Divinity whatsoever in the seat of the heavens may be propitious and kindly disposed to us and all who are placed under our rule And thus by this wholesome counsel and most upright provision we thought to arrange that no one whatsoever should be denied the opportunity to give his heart to the observance of the Christian religion, of that religion which he should think best for himself, so that the Supreme Deity, to whose worship we freely yield our hearts) may show in all things His usual favor and benevolence. Therefore, your Worship should know that it has pleased us to remove all conditions whatsoever, which were in the rescripts formerly given to you officially, concerning the Christians and now any one of these who wishes to observe Christian religion may do so freely and openly, without molestation. (The Edict continues by granting freedom of worship in location, a return of all money and goods and buildings or churches confiscated during the times of persecution.)

This text was translated at the University of Pennsylvania. Dept. of History: *Translations and Reprints from the Original Sources of European history,* (Philadelphia, University of Pennsylvania Press [1897?-1907?]), Vol. 4:, 1, pp. 28-30. This text is part of the Internet Medieval Source Book. The Sourcebook is a collection of public domain and copy-permitted texts related to medieval and Byzantine history.

(3) Athanasius - 296-373

Athanasius is one of the giants of Christian history because of his part in defining the doctrine of the Trinity in the Arian struggles. As a deacon of the Church at Alexandria, he went with his bishop, Alexander to the Council of Nicaea in 325. He succeeded Alexander as bishop in 328. When the Emperor got involved in the affairs of the Church it resulted in his exile on 5 different occasions. His basic theological viewpoint was that Christ was 'made man that we might be made divine'. Athansius' argument against the Arians was that if Christ was a created being and less than God then He could not be our Savior. Only God could restore man to communion with Himself. For this reason he defended Nicaea's definition of Christ as of the same substance with God, and Nicaea's rejection of Arianism. Most of Athanasius' writings are aimed at opposing Arianism. His Easter Letter 39 in 367 is the earliest witness to the 27 book New Testament Canon.

(4) Social Works

All through the 300's the Church was the only helper of the poor. They built hospitals, orphanages, houses for strangers, and they cared for the widows. Although the deeds were all done with good intentions, they focused on the needs of the people and not on proclaiming the gospel.

(5) Constantius and the Church - 337-361

The three sons of Constantine, Constantine II, Constantius, and Constans, divided up the Empire on his death in 337. After years of fighting and political intrigue,

Constantius became the sole ruler of a united kingdom in 353, with increasing inclinations towards Arianism. He finally forced an anti-Nicene creed upon reluctant bishops while securing Athanasius' condemnation. The climax of imperial intervention came at Milan in 355. Certain bishops were summoned before Constantius at his palace and ordered to condemn Athanasius. When they dared to appeal to the canons of the Church, the Emperor replied, "Whatever I will, shall be regarded as a canon ... Either obey of go into exile!"

By 358 Athanasius is convinced that the Emperor has gone too far... "When did a judgment of the Church receive its validity from the Emperor? There have been many councils held until the present and many judgments passed by the Church; but the Church leaders never sought the consent of the Emperor for them nor did the Emperor busy himself with the affairs of the Church."

In 356 Constantius decreed that pagan temples should be closed and prohibited sacrifices on pain of death, yet Athansius considered him to be worse than Saul, Ahab or Pilate. Indeed, he considered Constantius to be the herald of the antichrist. For the sake of unity, Constantius sacrificed truth and liberty, thus further eroding the truths known and practiced by the Early Church.

(6) Theodasius - 379-392

As the Church increased in social and imperial acceptance, the Church began filling up with people who became 'Christians' for the sake of prestige. In 380 Emperor Theodasius decreed that all subjects of the Empire MUST accept the Christian faith. Those who did not were now considered outlaws or criminals. In 391 another decree by Theodasius was directed towards pagan temples and idols, destroying them right and left as the tide of persecution turned. In this atmosphere it seemed that the Church had finally become victorious.

(7) Compromise in Worship - 392-397

As the Churches overnight filled with those seeking to escape persecution, severe pressure started being exerted against those adherents to truth and the fundamentals of the gospel. Compromise was in the air. The 'new converts' were really unconverted, having joined the Church to obey the law and not because they had repented of their sins and received Christ by faith. Because the unsaved did not know God they also didn't know how to worship God in Spirit and in truth.

Liturgies, or ritual speeches, and forms of prayers were produced so that the 'new converts' could participate. Choirs were introduced and hymns written so that a special group could maintain the sound of worship. Buildings became larger and more decorative. Church walls were covered with tapestries and paintings. Dignity and impressiveness were brought into the services so that the 'new converts' would be impressed.

The 'new converts' who had been accustomed to worshipping gods or sacred places quickly gravitated to the worship of saints, particularly Mary. Instead of idols or objects of worship they venerated pictures of saints and the crucifix.

Over time, the 'new converts' that could not trust in a God they did not know began to trust in the bishop that they could see. The bishop's word became law.

(8) The Roman Church Rules

The Western Church became more and more powerful as the Bishop of Rome became more influential. The Bishop of Rome began to be recognized as the Head of the Church in 440 with Pope (Bishop) Leo. When the Roman Empire fell in 476, the Roman Bishop (in Latin - Pope) took control of the civil government as well as the Church.

b. The Formation of the New Testament – 397 AD

Halley's Bible Handbook states that in the days of Christ there was in the literature of the Jewish nation a group of writings called *The Scriptures*, now called the Old Testament, which the people commonly regarded as having come from God. They called it *The Word of God*. As the writings of the Apostles appeared, they were added to these Jewish *Scriptures*, and were held in the same sacred regard.

There are hints in the New Testament itself that, while the Apostles were yet living, under their own supervision, collections of their writings began to be made for the Churches, and placed with the Old Testament as *The Word of God*.

Throughout the first and second century the Old Testament in Greek, called the *Septuagint*, was read in the Churches. Many Churches also read letters by different authors, such as Paul, Barnabas, and Peter. Many desired a recognized group of writings that could be elevated to the same level as the Old Testament. By about 200, according to the witness of a Muratorian fragment, Western Christianity had what they considered a New Testament *canon* that contained 23 books.

Eusebius (264-340), bishop of Caesarea and Church historian, lived through and was imprisoned during Diocletian's Great Persecution. That persecution was Rome's final attempt to blot out Christians, their faith, and their Scriptures. For ten years Scriptures were hunted by the agents of Rome, and burned in public market places. Eusebius became Constantine's chief religious advisor. One of Constantine's first acts on ascending the throne was to order, for the Churches in Constantinople, fifty Bibles to be prepared under the direction of Eusebius, by skillful copyists, on the finest vellum, and to be delivered by royal carriages from Caesarea to Constantinople.

Eusebius extensively researched the history of each book and their general acceptability amongst the Churches. In his *Church History,* he speaks of four classes of books.

(1) Those **universally** accepted.

(2) Those **disputed** books; James, II Peter, Jude, II & III John.

(3) Those **spurious**; like the *Acts of Paul, Shepherd of Hermas, and The Didache.*

(4) Those **forgeries of heretics;** like the *Gospel of Peter and the Acts of John.*

Throughout the first three centuries different parts of the Church also used a number of Jewish writings not found in the Old Testament. Most of these, such as the Wisdom of Solomon and Ecclesiasticus, were included in the *Septuagint* and are now known as the *Apocrapha*. There is much argument about how far they were given a status equal to the books of the Hebrew Bible. In the West, largely through Augustine's (354-430) influence (but against Jerome's - 345-420 - arguments), they later became accepted as part of the Scriptures. The East continued to recognize only the Hebrew books.

The Council of Carthage in 397 gave its formal ratification to the 27 books of the New Testament that did not include the *Apocrapha.*

c. **The Fall of Rome - 476**

To describe the Fall of Rome, is really to describe the fall of the Roman Empire in the West. The Eastern Empire, based in Constantinople or "East Rome", survived for another 1,000 years. Although the underlying reasons for the fall of the Western Empire are still disputed, the immediate cause was the Germanic invasions of the fifth century.

Germanic tribes had threatened the Roman frontier for several centuries. According to Eerdmans though, the tribes who finally destroyed the Western Empire were new to the Romans – Goths, Vandals, Burgundians, Lombards and others. Most important of these were the Goths, who began to attack the Empire about the middle of the third century. The Visogoths, the western branch of the Goths, occupied the Roman province of Dacia and forced the Emperor Aurelian to abandon it in 271.

Roman prisoners taken on raids into the Empire

introduced the Visogoths to Christianity during their occupation of Dacia. About the end of Constantine's reign, Ulfila, a descendant of one of the Christian Roman prisoners, was consecrated head of the Christian community there by an Arian bishop. The Visogoths, therefore, became Arian Christians and eventually spread their particular kind of Christianity to most of the other German tribes on the border of the Empire. Ulfila's most important achievement was the translation of the Scriptures into the Gothic language, for which task he had to invent a Gothic alphabet.

In 395 the Empire was divided between Arcadius and Honorius, the two young sons of Theodosius. Alaric, the new king of the Visogoths, began to exploit the differences that now developed between the East and West. Encouraged, apparently, by Constantinople, he invaded Italy in 401. On the night of 24 August 410, Alaric stormed the walls of Rome in a surprise attack and pillaged the city for three days. The event had little permanent effect on the Empire since Alaric soon abandoned the city; but the psychological blow was enormous.

For the first time in 800 years a foreign enemy had taken Rome. Jerome, far away in his monastery at Bethlehem, wept: 'The city which has taken the whole world is itself taken!'

Augustine of Hippo, the great North African bishop and theologian countered the accusation that Rome had fallen due to its rejection of their ancestral gods in his book *The City of God*. Augustine wrote that within the Roman Empire two 'cities' were intertwined: the City of God, the community of true Christians living according to God's law, and the City of Man, pagan society following its own desires and seeking material gain. Such a community could only come to a disastrous end. The City of God alone is eternal, yet the two cities will coexist inseparably until the end of the world.

When the Visogoths returned to Gaul they came under heavy attacks by barbarian tribes. Attila the Hun is possibly the most famous of the barbarian tribal-kings. In 452 Attila invaded Italy but was persuaded to withdraw - according to tradition, by a Roman delegation led by Pope Leo I. Meanwhile another Germanic people, the Vandals led by Gaiseric, had crossed from Spain into North Africa in 429, and by 435 controlled much of the coast.

They mastered the sea and in 455 dared to attack Rome itself. The Romans were unprepared and leaderless. It is reported that Leo again saved Rome by pleading with Gaiseric for restraint in his 14-day sack of the city. The next two decades were filled with wars against the Vandals and complicated intrigues, in which puppet emperors were set up and deposed at will by barbarian generals. Eventually, the barbarian Roman army in Italy revolted

3. **The Rejection of Truth - Middle Ages - 590 to 1517 AD**

   a. **590 - 1073**

   This was a period where the Papacy was continuing to gain power and rise to supremacy. This period ended with Gregory VII of Hilderbrand, who was considered to have the greatest power of any Pope.

   b. **1073 - 1294**

   This was the age of the greatest power of the Papacy as a whole. It was also actually the darkest period for the true Church. There is very little evidence in the Church during this period of truth and worship.

   God did not allow the light of the gospel to be extinguished. God always kept a remnant of true believers for Himself - even in the midst of the darkest hour!

   c. **1294 - 1517**

   During this period the power of the Papacy declined. Small groups started springing up everywhere in resistance to the Papacy and the Roman Catholic (Universal) Church. This period ended with the revival of learning - the Renaissance. Here we see the seeds of truth beginning to spring up. God begins to set the stage for the restoration of truth, or the reformation.

   (1) John Wycliffe - 1324-1384

   He was called the "Morning Star of the Reformation", paving the way for the others who would follow. In 1380 he translated the New Testament into the common English language, and in 1384 the Old Testament with the aid of his friends immediately before his death. He advocated the people's right to read the BIBLE. He attacked transubstantiation (where the bread and wine are transformed into the veritable body and blood of Christ) and preached that the elements should be regarded as symbols. He also urged that Church services should be simple and patterned after the New Testament. He preached against the Priesthood and attacked articular confessions.

(2) The Lollards

In the 1400's, these were the followers of Wycliffe who were humble, itinerant preachers. Beginning in Oxford and spreading to Leicestershire these followers became known as Lollards, which may mean 'mutterer' or 'mumbler'. They proclaimed Christ throughout England and started a rebellion against Rome. They were known as 'poor priests' as they traveled about England believing that the main task of a priest was to preach, and that the Bible should be available to everyone in his own language. This desire to return to the truths of the WORD OF GOD actually formed the foundation for what was to follow. At the height of their influence it was estimated that over 50% of the population of England were either Lollards or in sympathy with them. It was a remarkable move of the Holy Spirit - something not seen in hundreds of years. They were even more outspoken than Wycliffe was about their opposition to Rome.

(3) Johann Gutenberg   1400-1468

Eerdmans states that, "A whole new dimension in the history of books, scholarship and education opened up with the invention of printing - sometimes called Germany's chief contribution to the Renaissance. The art of printing from hand-cut wooden blocks was invented in Asia about the fifth century, and the first known printed book was produced by this means in China in 868. But Europe had to wait until the middle of the fifteenth century for the art to be rediscovered and developed. About 1445 Johann Gutenberg began to pioneer with movable metal type at Mainz in Germany, and- significantly- the first complete book known to have been printed in the Christian world was the Bible in 1456." The printing press was a momentous invention and a revolutionary step forward in technology.

TRUTH RESTORED - Modern Period - 1517 to the present

1. Truths Restored in the 16th Century

a. Martin Luther - 1483-1546

More books have been written about Luther, the great German Reformer, than about any other figure in history, except Christ. Martin Luther, whose name at birth was Martin Luder - later changing his name to the more academically acceptable Luther, was born in Eisleben, Germany in 1483. As a schoolboy, Luther preferred music to any other subject, and he became proficient at playing the lute. He gave away his lute when he entered the monastic cloister at the age of 21. Before he became a friar though, Luther was well on his way to becoming a lawyer. He earned both his bachelor's and master's degrees in the shortest possible time. It wasn't until he was 20 that he even saw his first Bible. While walking to law school in 1505, Luther encountered a frightening thunderstorm. During the storm he cried out in fear, "Help me, St. Anna! I will become a monk." He kept his vow and joined the Augustinian Hermits in Erfurt. Luther was ordained in 1507. While celebrating his first Mass he trembled so much he nearly dropped the bread and cup. He became so terrified of the presence of Christ in the sacrament that he tried to run from the altar. Soon after this he was sent to the University of Wittenburg to teach moral theology. In 1510-11 he visited Rome on business for his order, and in 1512 became a doctor of theology and professor of biblical studies at Wittenburg.

After a long spiritual battle Luther finally came to understand the nature of the righteousness of God. He then rejected all theology based solely on tradition, and began emphasizing the need for a personal understanding and experience of God's Word, which he insisted is the Church's sole authority. He believed that all our actions stem from God. The discovery that God spares the sinner was always decisive for him. He also discovered that we are justified not by our deeds, but by faith alone. In 1514 he began to publicly criticize the abuse and selling of indulgences. In 1517 Luther's views became widely known when he posted his *95 Theses* on the church door at Wittenburg.

Opposition quickly arose all around him, but Luther became even firmer. In July 1519, during a disputation at Leipzig with Eck, his sharpest opponent, Luther denied the supremacy of the pope and the infallibility of general councils. He burned the papal order that threatened his excommunication. In 1520 through 1521 Luther was the rage in

Germany. Posters of Luther (single-sheet woodcuts) sold out as soon as they went on sale, and many more were pinned up in public places.

Excommunication from the Roman Catholic Church finally came in 1521 and Luther spent the rest of his life as an outlaw. At the Diet of Worms (a general council of the church) in April 1521 he made this famous response to his critics.

Your Imperial Majesty and Your Lordships demand a simple answer. Here it is, plain and unvarnished. Unless I am convicted of error by the testimony of Scripture or (since I put no trust in the unsupported authority of pope or of councils, since it is plain that they have often erred and often contradicted themselves) by manifest reasoning I stand convicted by the Scriptures to which I have appealed, and my conscience is taken captive by God's word, I cannot and will not recant anything. For to act against our conscience is neither safe for us, nor open to us. On this I take my stand. I can do no other. God help me. Amen.

In 1522 he set about to reform public worship by freeing the mass from rigid forms. He stressed preaching the Word, the communion and congregational singing. By the end of his life in 1546, Martin Luther had written 60,000 pages, yet his hope was that "all my books would disappear and the Holy Scriptures alone be read."

[From Eerdmans Handbook to the History of Christianity & Fascinating Facts from the pages of Christian History]

b. **3 Principles of the Reformation**

(1) God's Word is Authoritative - **2 Pet. 1:3-4, 19-21**

(2) Salvation is by Grace Alone - **Rom. 1:16-17**

(3) Every Believer is a Priest - **1 Pet. 2:9**

c. **Phillip Melanchton - 1497-1560**

On Luther's death, Phillip Melanchton (1497-1560) took over the theological leadership of the movement he had begun. Melanchton taught Greek, first in Tubingen, then at the University of Wittenburg. There, in 1518, he met Luther. This decisive encounter changed Melanchton from a humanist into a theologian and a reformer. With his gift for logical

104

consistency and wide knowledge of history, Melanchton's influence on Protestantism was in certain ways even greater than Luther's. In 1519 Melanchton publicly supported Luther at the Leipzig Disputation. When Luther was away from Wittenburg, Phillip represented and defended him. In 1521 he wrote a book that described clearly the teachings of the Reformation, entitled *Commonplaces*. He was also responsible for the *Augsburg Confession* (1530), which remains the chief statement of faith in the Lutheran churches.

d. Huldreich Zwingli - 1484-1531

Historically the first mention of Zwingli was when he, as a Catholic priest, became the chaplain to the Swiss mercenary forces at the battle of Novara in 1513. Zwingli met Erasmus in 1515 and was deeply influenced. He soon began to develop evangelical beliefs as he reflected on the abuses of the Catholic Church. In 1518 he was made the people's priest at the Great Minster in Zurich, Switzerland. He lectured on the New Testament and began to reform Zurich, working carefully with the city council. In 1522 he secretly married Anna Meyer who bore him four children. The Catholic bishop of Constance attempted to stop Zwingli and his beliefs, but Zwingli overcame him in two public debates in 1523. He continued to win debates until he ran up against Luther when they deadlocked over the issue of the Eucharist (communion) in 1529. As a result the Swiss reform movement lost the support of the German princes. The Catholics sent an army against Zurich, and Zwingli died at the battle of Kappel. Zwingli had rejected much of Catholicism, Lutheranism ad Anabaptism but was influenced by Erasmus. He was the first of the reformed theologians, yet believed that Christ was spiritually present at the Eucharist and that the secular ruler had a right to act in church matters. Zwingli's death halted the reformation movement in German-speaking Switzerland.

e. Anabaptists - 1523

The Anabaptists made the most radical attempt of the Reformation era to renew the Church. The difficulty in studying this movement is that it did not consist of just one group or surround one leader. All parts of this movement did reject infant baptism and began baptizing adults upon their confession of faith. They

105

never accepted the label "Anabaptists" which meant "Re-baptizer" - because it was a term of reproach coined by their opponents. To those in this movement the fundamental issue was not baptism but the role of the civil government within the church. Late in 1523 intense debate broke out over this issue in Zurich. At that time it became clear that the Zurich city council was unwilling to bring about the religious changes that the theologians believed were called for by scriptures. Zwingli had felt that one should wait and try to persuade the authorities by preaching. On January 21, 1525 the city council of Zurich forbade the radicals to assemble and discuss their views. That evening, in the neighboring village of Zollikon, 'praying that God would grant them to do His divine will and that He would show them mercy,' the radicals met, baptized each other, and so became the first free church of modern times. This movement spread rapidly throughout German speaking Europe.

In 1527 the growing movement attempted to hold a synod or meeting to determine a list of statements they could agree on. This document became known as the "Brotherly Union." By 1540 the movement has settled on 7 basic issues that were commonly agreed upon.

(1) They rejected the swearing of oaths. For them there could be no levels of truth.

(2) They acted as pacifists based on the principle of love. They would neither go to war, nor take part in coercion by the state.

(3) They were committed to not just reforming the church, but to its *restoration*. They wanted to see the church restored to what they saw in the New Testament church with its vigor and faithfulness, not just being a wealthy and powerful institution, but a brotherhood - a family of faith.

(4) They believed in the 'congregational' view of church authority towards which both Luther and Zwingli had inclined in their earliest reforming years. In deciding matters of doctrine, the authority of Scripture was to be interpreted, not by a dogmatic tradition or by an ecclesiastical leader, but by the consensus of the local gathering in which all could speak, and listen critically.

(5) They believed that all members were to be

believers, baptized voluntarily as adults upon confession of faith.

(6) They insisted on the separation of church and state. They claimed that Christians were a "free, unforced, uncompelled people."

(7) They also believed the church was distinct from society, even if society claimed to be Christian. True followers were a pilgrim people - and his church was an association of perpetual aliens.

f. John Calvin - 1509-1564

On July 27, 1509, at Noyon, Picardy in northern France, Jean Cauvin (better known as John Calvin) was born. His father Gerard was highly esteemed by most of the nobility in the district and has become the financial secretary to the resident bishop. Calvin was a diligent student and received a very liberal education. His father hoped that he would become a priest. However, it was more obvious that the legal profession was a more certain road to wealth, and his father later encouraged him to study law. Calvin, in obedience to his father's wishes, did pursue legal studies at Orleans, Bourges and the University of Paris. His first published book was an academic commentary on the ancient philosopher Seneca.

Apparently Calvin was a devoted Catholic, with strong attachments to the papal system. In Paris, the young Calvin became acquainted with the teachings of Luther, although he never did meet him. About 1533 he experienced a sudden conversion that he described in this way: "God subdued and brought my heart to docility. It was more hardened against such matters than was to be expected in such a young man." He broke with Roman Catholicism leaving France and living as an exile in Basle. He began to formulate his theology, and in 1536, before his 27th birthday, published the first edition of *The Institution of the Christian Religion* (better known as the *Institutes*). It was a brief, clear defense of Reformation beliefs.

Calvin felt that time was such a precious commodity that he always tried to never waste any of it. Even on his deathbed, his friends pleaded with him to refrain from his labors to which he replied, "What! Would you have the Lord find me idle when He comes?" In 1564 he died of a combination of various diseases. He seemed to have known that his death was near because in April of that year he dictated his last will and testament.

Calvin was strongly influenced by Lutheranism doctrinally. For Calvin, all knowledge of God and man is to be found only in the Word of God. We can only know God if he chooses to be known. Pardon and salvation are possible only through the free working of the grace of God. Calvin claimed that even before creation, "God chose some of his creatures for salvation and others for destruction." The well-known "five points of Calvinism" are often summarized by the simple acrostic "**TULIP**":

(1) **T**otal depravity - man's whole nature was ruined by sin; he is completely helpless in regard to salvation.

(2) **U**nconditional election - God chose a remnant from among mankind according to His sovereign will.

(3) **L**imited redemption - Christ's atoning death, burial, and resurrection applies only to the elect.

(4) **I**rresistible regenerating grace - All those whom God has elected will be called, justified, and will be carried to completion of salvation through the initiative of God.

(5) **P**erseverance of the elect - All those in whom God has initiated salvation will continue; they are kept eternally secure by God.

{Once saved, always saved}

These points are closely intertwined and depend upon one another. Many people opposed Calvin's views and claimed that they could lead to the idea that grace allows one to do whatever they wish since their salvation is eternally secure in Christ.

The foremost opponent to Calvinism was a Dutch theologian named **Jacob Arminius (1560-1609)**. Arminius did not speak and write as much as his followers later published in his name. The five counterpoints of Arminianism attempted to restore an emphasis on man's free will in response to God's persuading grace:

(1) God determined before the foundation of the world to save those who believe on Christ and persevere in faith until the end.

(2) Christ's redemption is for all, but only those who will believe actually appropriate the benefits of salvation.

108

(3) Sinful man must be born again and renewed before he can understand, think, will, or do anything God considers good.

(4) Apart from God's grace, man is helpless; but it is up to him whether or not to respond to God's grace - it is not irresistible.

(5) Victory over sin becomes available to all who are made partakers of Christ by faith; true believers will be overcomers.

{Backsliders will perish}

Both sides of this argument are based on Scripture. The reason this can be is that in Scripture this doctrine is paradoxical. Both emphases are there. Calvinism exalts the grace of God as the only source of salvation - and so does the Bible. Arminianism emphasizes man's free will and responsibility - and so does the Bible.

The practical solution lies in avoiding the unscriptural extremes of either view, and in refraining from setting one view squarely against the other. For example: overemphasis of God's sovereignty and grace in salvation may lead to careless living, for if a person is led to believe that his conduct and attitude have nothing to do with his salvation, he may become negligent. On the other hand, overemphasis of man's free will and responsibility, in reaction against Calvinism, may bring people under the bondage of legalism and rob them of all assurance. Lawlessness and legalism - these are the two extremes to be avoided. Balance is essential!

John Wesley (1703 – 1791), the founder of the Methodist movement, writes the following.

There are two points in debate: 1- Unconditional Election. 2- Irresistible Grace.

1- With regard to the Unconditional Election, I believe;

- That God, before the foundation of the world, did unconditionally elect certain persons to do certain works, as Paul was to preach the gospel;

- That He has unconditionally elected some nations to receive peculiar privileges; the Jewish nation in particular;

- That He has unconditionally elected some

nations to hear the gospel, as England and Scotland have now, and many others in past ages;

- That He has unconditionally elected some persons to many peculiar advantages, with regard to both temporal and spiritual things;

- And I do not deny (though I cannot prove it is so)

  - That He has unconditionally elected some persons to eternal glory.

- But I cannot believe -

  - That all those who are not thus elected to glory must perish everlastingly; or

  - That there is one soul on earth who has not ever had a possibility of escaping eternal damnation.

2- With regard to Irresistible Grace, I believe -

- That the grace which brings faith, and thereby salvation, into the soul, is irresistible at that moment;

- That most believers may remember some time when God did irresistibly convince them of sin;

- That most believers so at sometimes find God irresistibly acting upon their souls;

- Yet I believe, that the grace of God, both before and after those moments, may be and hath been resisted; and that in general it does not act irresistibly, but we must comply therewith or may not.

- And I do not deny - That in some souls the grace of God is so far irresistible, that they cannot but believe and be finally saved.

- But I cannot believe - That all must be damned, in whom it does not thus irresistibly work; or That there is one soul on earth, who has not, and never had any other grace, than such as does in fact increase his damnation, and was designated of God to do so.

Whosoever will - Rev. 22:17; Isa. 55:1; John 7:37-38

Predestination - Eph. 1:4-5; Rom. 8:29 (foreknowledge precedes predestination)

g. John Knox - 1515?-1572

The life of John Knox is the really the story of Protestantism in Scotland. The Reformation was slow in coming to Scotland. Patrick Hamilton (1504?-1528), who had visited Wittenberg and studied in Marburg, preached Lutheran doctrine, and was burned on February 29, 1528. The cause grew slowly. In 1534 and 1540 there were other executions. Yet, in 1543 the Scottish Parliament authorized the reading and translation of the Bible. It was but a temporary phase, due to English influence, and by 1544 Cardinal Beaton and the French party (a strong force politically as Scotland withstood many attempts of English domination with their help) were employing strong repression. Chief of the preachers at this time was George Wishart (1513?-1546), who was burned by the Cardinal Beaton on March 2, 1546. On May 29 Beaton himself was brutally murdered, partly in revenge for Wishart's death and partly out of hostility to his French policy. The murderers gained possession of the castle of St. Andrews and rallied their sympathizers there. In 1547 a hunted Protestant preacher, apparently a convert and certainly a friend of Wishart, took refuge with them and became their spiritual teacher. This was John Knox, who was to become the hero of the Scottish reformation.

Born in or near Haddington, between 1505 and 1515, Knox's early career was obscure. He was certainly ordained to the priesthood, but when Wishart was arrested he was with that martyr, and prepared to defend him. French forces sent to quell the uprising in St. Andrews forced its surrender and carried Knox to France to endure 19 months of cruel life as a galley-slave. Released at length, he made his way to England, then under the Protestant government ruling in the name of Edward VI, became one of the royal chaplains. When Mary of Lorraine ascended the throne in 1554 Knox was compelled to flee to Geneva, where he became an ardent disciple of Calvin.

In 1555 Knox dared to return to Scotland and preached for six months, but the situation was not yet ripe for revolt so he returned to Geneva to become the pastor of the English-speaking refugees there. His preaching germinated even in his absence though and on December 3, 1557, a number of Protestant and anti-French nobles in Scotland entered into a

111

covenant to "establish the most blessed Word of God and His congregation" - from which they were nicknamed "The Lords of the Congregation."

Additional fuel was given to this dissent by the marriage of Mary "Queen of Scots" to the French heir on April 24, 1558. Scotland now seemed a province of France. The time now seemed ripe for Knox and he returned to Scotland on May 2, 1559, with the ringing anthem of "Give me Scotland or I die!" By 1560 Knox had created a Calvinistic confession of faith that adopted as the creed of the realm by the Scottish Parliament. They also abolished papal jurisdiction and forbade the mass under pain of death.

Knox and his associates now proceeded to formalize their work. In 1561 the *First Book of discipline* was presented to Parliament. It was an amazing document, attempting to apply the system worked out by Calvin to a whole kingdom, though the full Presbyterian system was far from thoroughly developed. In each parish there would be a minister and elders holding office with the consent of the congregation. Ministers and elders constituted the disciplinary board - the "session" - with power of excommunication. In the larger towns were to be meetings for discussion, out of which "presbyteries" were to grow; over groups of ministers and congregations were "synods" and over all these the "General Assembly." The *Book* also suggested ways of national education and for the relief of the poor. These final statements caused division in the Parliament so that it was not adopted in force. All observances not having Scriptural authority were swept away. Sunday was the only remaining holy day. At his death in November of 1572, John Knox had influenced not merely the religion but the character of Scotland more than any other man in history.

2. Truths Restored in the 17th Century

a. Anglican - Episcopal Church

According to the Encarta Encyclopedia, the **Church of England** or **Anglican Church**, the Christian church in England, dates from the introduction of Christianity into that country. (Currently this denomination is known in the United States as the Episcopal Church.) More specifically, it is the branch of the Christian church that, since the Reformation, has been the established Church of England. The earliest unquestioned historical evidence of an organized Christian church in England is found in the writings of such early Christian fathers as Tertullian and Origen in the first years of the 3rd century, although the first Christian communities probably were established some decades earlier. Three English bishops are known to have been present at the Council of Arles in 314. Others attended the Council of Sardica in 347 and that of Ariminum in 360, and a number of references to the church in Roman Britain are found in the writings of 4th-century Christian fathers.

The ritual and discipline of the early English church were largely introduced by the Celtic and Gallic missionaries and monks, but after the arrival of St. Augustine and his missionary companions from Rome, in 597, and the ensuing fusion of Celtic and Roman influences, the Celtic forms gradually gave way to the liturgy and practices of the Roman West. During the next four centuries, the church in Saxon England exhibited the same lines of growth and development that characterized the church everywhere in the early Middle Ages. After the Norman Conquest (1066), continental influence in England strengthened the connections between the English church and the papacy. The vigorous assertions of power successfully made by popes from Gregory VII to Innocent III between the late 11th and the early 13th centuries were felt in England, as elsewhere, and clerical influence and privilege were widely extended in secular affairs.

b. **Separatists**

Separatists were dissenters who withdrew from the Church of England during the 16th and 17th centuries because of their dissatisfaction with the ritual used in worship and with the state control of religion in England. The English clergyman Robert Browne was influential among them, and his followers came to be known as Brownists. His writings contain perhaps the earliest statement of Congregational principles. In the 17th century the Separatists became known as Independents; their congregational system was brought to America by the Pilgrims.

c. **Pilgrims**

Pilgrims, early English settlers who founded Plymouth Colony, the first permanent settlement in

113

New England. They were originally known as the Forefathers or Founders; the term *Pilgrim* was first used in the writings of colonist William Bradford.

Among the early Pilgrims was a group of Separatists. In 1606 William Brewster led a group of Separatists to Leiden, the Netherlands, to escape religious persecution in England. After living in Leiden for more than ten years, some members of the group voted to immigrate to America. The voyage was financed by a group of London investors who were promised produce from America in exchange for their assistance. On September 16, 1620, these Separatists were part of a group numbering 102 men, women, and children who left Plymouth, England, for America on the *Mayflower*.

On November 21, the *Mayflower* dropped anchor in the sheltered harbor off the site of present-day Provincetown, Massachusetts. They landed on the site of Plymouth Colony the following December 21, a date that is celebrated in New England as Forefathers' Day. The Pilgrims established a government and created the Mayflower Compact, the first constitution written in America.

d. John Robinson - 1576-1625

He was known as the leader of the "Pilgrim Fathers." In his farewell address to the Pilgrim Fathers on their departure from England on the Mayflower he said the following. **"If God reveals anything to you by another instrument, be as ready to receive it as ever you were to receive any truth by my ministry, for I am persuaded that the Lord has more truth yet to break forth out of His Holy Word."** He eventually also immigrated to New England.

e. Bradford, William - 1590-1657

The Encarta Encyclopedia states that he was one of the Pilgrim leaders and American colonial governor, born in Austerfield, Yorkshire, England. In 1606 he joined the Separatists. Three years later, in search of freedom of worship, he went with them to Holland, where he became an apprentice to a silk manufacturer. Bradford sailed on the Mayflower in 1620, and after his arrival in America he helped found Plymouth Colony. In April 1621 he succeeded Governor John Carver as chief executive of Plymouth Colony. Except for five years, Bradford served as governor almost continuously from 1621 through 1656, having been reelected 30 times. In

1621 he negotiated a treaty with Massasoit, the chief of the Wampanoag tribe. Under the treaty, which was vital to the maintenance and growth of the colony, Massasoit disavowed Native American claims to the Plymouth area and pledged peace with the colonists. The first Thanksgiving Day celebration in New England was organized by Bradford in 1621. Bradford was a delegate on four occasions to the New England Confederation, of which he was twice elected president. His *History of Plimoth Plantation, 1620-1647,* was published in 1856, 200 years after his death. The book is an important source of information about the early settlers.

f. Puritanism

This was a movement arising within the Church of England in the latter part of the 16th century, which sought to carry the reformation of that church beyond the point represented by the Elizabethan settlement (1559), an attempt to establish a middle course between Roman Catholicism and the ideas of the Protestant reformers. The term *Puritanism* is also used in a broader sense to refer to attitudes and values considered characteristic of the Puritans. Thus, the Separatists in the 16th century, the Quakers in the 17th century, and Nonconformists after the Restoration may be called Puritans, although they were no longer part of the established church. The founders of New England are also commonly called Puritans.

Even within the Church of England, a precise definition of Puritanism is elusive. The leading Puritan clergyman in Elizabeth's reign was **Thomas Cartwright**, who denied he was one. He is particularly remembered for his advocacy of presbyterianism; but Puritanism cannot be strictly identified with presbyterianism, because a major segment of the movement eventually adopted congregationalism. The essence of Puritanism is in the intensity of the Puritan's commitment to a morality, a form of worship, and a civil society strictly conforming to God's commandments.

Puritan theology is a version of Calvinism. It asserts the basic sinfulness of humankind; but it also declares that by an eternal decree God has determined that some will be saved through the righteousness of Christ despite their sins. No one can be certain in this life what his or her eternal destiny will be. Nevertheless, the experience of conversion, in which the Holy Spirit touches the soul, so that the inward bias of the heart is turned from sinfulness to holiness, is at least some indication that one is of the elect.

g. Congregationalism

Congregationalism is a form of church government in which each individual congregation or local church is fully self-governing.

Congregationalism as a Generic Term

In this sense, **Congregationalism** contrasts with other forms, such as Episcopacy and Presbyterianism. **Episcopacy** asserts that authority in the church is exercised by the order of bishops. **Presbyterianism** is organized into a hierarchical structure, which, in ascending order of its parts, consists of the local congregation, the presbytery (representing a number of congregations), the regional synod, and an over-all general assembly. Each of these Presbyterian bodies exercises a certain amount of authority over its constituent bodies. The differences among these forms may be illustrated by the power to ordain. In episcopacy, it rests with the bishops; in Presbyterianism, it is by action of the presbytery; but in congregationalism, the local church may ordain its own minister. Congregationalism is a group of many religious bodies besides those that have used the term *congregational* in the name of the denomination. These include the Baptists, the Unitarians, and churches of the Campbellite tradition such as the Christian Church (Disciples of Christ).

3. Truths Restored in the 18th Century

a. Pietism

Pietism, originally, a German Lutheran reform movement of the 17th and 18th centuries which emphasized individual conversion, "living faith," and the fruits of faith in daily life. The name Pietism is derived from the *collegia pietatis* (informal devotional meetings) organized by Philipp Jakob Spener while he was a pastor in Frankfurt. First held in Spener's home on Sunday afternoons, these meetings soon became popular across Germany. Participants did not separate from the established church and its worship but tried to change the church from within. They held prayer meetings, studied the Bible individually and in small groups, and led a disciplined Christian life. Claiming that faith is not the acceptance of correct theological propositions but trust in Christ, they insisted that pastors should have such faith in addition to their theological learning. Convinced that the world could be won for Christ through the conversion and Christian training of individuals, Pietists stressed the importance of education. Modern Pietists place emphasis on an ecumenical spirit, the "kingdom of God" and its realization in history, ethics, and personal Christian experience. [George Wolfgang Forell]

b. Edwards, Jonathan – 1703 - 1758

Jonathan Edwards was an American theologian and Congregational clergyman, whose sermons stirred the religious revival called the Great Awakening.

When Edwards was 26, his grandfather died, and the young man became pastor at Northampton. He was a firm believer in Calvinism and the doctrine of predestination and was a notable pulpit orator. The result of his 1734-35 sermons was a religious revival in which a great number of conversions were made; Edwards received 300 new members into his church. Some of the converted were so obsessed by his fiery descriptions of eternal damnation that they contemplated suicide. In 1740 the British evangelist George Whitefield visited Edwards.

Together, the two men were the focal point of a revival movement that became known as the Great Awakening and developed into a religious frenzy engulfing all New England. The conversions were characterized by convulsions and hysteria on the part of the converts. The harshness and appeal to religious fear in one of Edward's sermons, "Sinners in the Hands of an Angry God," caused his congregation to rise weeping and moaning from their seats. By 1742 the revival movement had grown out of control, and for the next 60 to 70 years it had the effect on American religion of preventing any attempt at a liberal interpretation of doctrine.

c. Whitefield, George – 1714 - 1770

Whitefield was born in Gloucester, England, and educated at Pembroke College, University of Oxford. During his undergraduate days Whitefield met John and Charles Wesley and joined the Holy Club, the members of which were known as Methodists. In 1736 Whitefield was ordained deacon in the Church of England and two years later followed the Wesley brothers to Savannah, Georgia, as a missionary. Shortly thereafter, Whitefield returned to England and was ordained a priest in the Anglican Church. Because of his unconventional manner of preaching and conducting services, many Church of England pulpits were closed to him; he therefore began to preach in the open air and attracted vast crowds by his eloquence. In 1739 he returned to America and participated with the American Congregational clergyman Jonathan Edwards in inaugurating the revival movement that later became known as the Great Awakening.

The extraordinary influence Whitefield exercised during his lifetime was attributable chiefly to his oratorical skill; he is said to have preached more than 18,000 sermons. His collected writings were published posthumously (7 vol., 1771-72).

d. Wesley, John – 1703 - 1791

Wesley was born in the rectory at Epworth, Lincolnshire, on June 17, 1703, the 15th child of the British clergyman Samuel Wesley. He was educated at Charterhouse School and Christ Church, University of Oxford. Ordained deacon in 1725 and admitted to the priesthood of the Church of England in 1728, John Wesley acted for a time as curate to his father. In 1729 he went into residence at Oxford as a fellow of Lincoln College. There he joined the Holy Club, a group of students that included his brother Charles Wesley and, later, George Whitefield. The club members adhered strictly and methodically to religious precepts and practices, among them visiting prisons and comforting the sick, and were thus derisively called "methodists" by their schoolmates.

Wesley attracted immense crowds virtually from the outset of his evangelical career. His success also was due, in part, to the fact that contemporary England was ready for a revivalist movement; the Anglican Church was seemingly unable to offer the kind of personal faith that people craved. Thus Wesley's emphasis on inner religion and his assurance that each person was accepted as a child of God had a tremendous popular appeal.

An indefatigable preacher and organizer, Wesley traveled about 5000 miles a year, delivering as many as four or five sermons a day and founding new societies.

e. The Great Awakening

This was a general revival of evangelical religion in

the American colonies, which reached its peak in the early 1740s. Local revivals had occurred previously, inspired by the teaching of such clergymen as the congregational theologian Jonathan Edwards. In 1739 and 1740 the English evangelist George Whitefield made extended tours along the Atlantic seaboard, attracting large crowds as he preached the necessity for sinners to be converted. Others followed his example of itinerant preaching, and many small local revivals merged into a general "great awakening."

Whitefield, the Presbyterian clergyman Gilbert Tennent, and other traveling revivalists were generally welcomed at first. They stimulated religious zeal, produced conversions, and increased church membership. Before long, however, the methods of the itinerants and the fervent emotionalism of the revival drew criticism, being seen by a large proportion of the settled clergy as a threat to the established order.

The Great Awakening had varied and to some degree contradictory effects on American religion. In New England, Calvinism was reinvigorated, and Jonathan Edwards emerged as the leading orthodox theologian. Opponents of the revival, however, began preaching against the orthodox doctrines of predestination, election, and original sin. The congregational clergyman Charles Chauncey of Boston, for instance, attacked revivalist excesses and began to advocate a theological liberalism that eventually developed into Unitarianism. In the Middle Colonies, on the other hand, many Scottish and Scotch-Irish Presbyterians reacted by reaffirming orthodox doctrine, which, they argued, was weakened by the revivalists' emphasis on religious experience.

In community after community, the Great Awakening produced tension, discord, and factional rivalry, so that whatever religious harmony and uniformity had existed was disrupted. Nevertheless, evangelical fervor drew supporters of the revival together, producing a sense of unity transcending denominational and political boundaries. The Great Awakening was thus a significant intercolonial movement, which contributed to a sense of American nationality before the American Revolution.

f. Moravians

The Encarta Encyclopedia states that historically, the

Moravians were Slavic tribes dwelling northeast of the Carpathian Mountains that were involved in the great migrations of Northern Europe. As these migrations took place, the western tribes eventually evolved as the Moravians, Poles, Czechs, and Slovaks; the southern tribes as the Serbs, Croats, Slovenes, and the Slavicized Bulgers; and the eastern tribes as the modern Russians, Ukrainians, and Belarusians.

Zinzendorf, Nikolaus Ludwig, Graf von (1700-60), was a German religious reformer who led the Renewed Church of the Unity of the Brethren, also known as the Moravian Church. Zinzendorf was born in Dresden, Saxony, and was brought up by his grandmother, who was a member of the Pietists movement. He studied law at the University of Wittenberg. In 1722 Zinzendorf granted refuge on his estate in Upper Lusatia to a group of Moravians of the persecuted Bohemian Brethren. Their community, called Herrnhut, became a refuge for the Brethren from other lands and for members of other persecuted Protestant sects.

The Brethren functioned for a time within the Lutheran church, of which Zinzendorf was a member. In 1727, however, they formed a new denomination, known as the Renewed Church of the Unity of the Brethren. Although opposed to the separation, Zinzendorf continued to lead the congregation. In 1734 he was ordained a Lutheran minister under an assumed name. Herrnhut missionaries meanwhile had been dispatched to many parts of the world. For the next ten years Zinzendorf traveled widely, founding Moravian congregations in the Netherlands, England, Ireland, Germany, and the Russian provinces of Estonia and Livonia. He visited the American colonies in 1741 and during the next two years helped to establish several Moravian communities in Pennsylvania, including Bethlehem. In addition, he promoted missionary work among the Native Americans. He spent his final years in Herrnhut and died there on May 9, 1760.

Zinzendorf taught and practiced fervent devotion to Jesus Christ, through whom alone, he believed, God had revealed himself to humankind. He exalted the importance of full emotional participation in worship and insisted that reason has no place in religion. He was also, however, a strong advocate of church discipline. His writings include about 2000 hymns, many sermons, and various polemical treatises.

Moravian Missionaries were to affect the world. By 1740 they had begun works in at least 10 countries, and had reached the Virgin Islands, Greenland, Surinam, the Gold Coast, North America and South Africa. Their self-sacrifice, love and total commitment to evangelization are unparalleled in the history of missions. Despite the group's small size, the Moravians sent out hundreds of missionaries in the eighteenth century - and inspired countless others.

Moravian Beliefs - The Moravians have no specific creed, but their tenets agree in substance with those incorporated in the Apostles' Creed and the Augsburg Confession. The Bible is the only guide to faith and conduct. Infant baptism is practiced, but full church membership requires only a voluntary profession of faith. Congregations follow a liturgical form of worship; many retain the love feast in imitation of the ancient agape. Special stress is placed on fellowship and missionary work. Moravian church music, especially singing, is known worldwide. The Moravian Church in America is noted for its unity.

g. **William Carey - 1761-1834**

In the 1700's cross-cultural evangelism stirred little, if any, interest. William Carey's missionary endeavors to the peoples of India earned him the title of the "Father of Modern Missions." He was born at Paulerspury, Northhamptonshire, the son of a parish clerk and schoolmaster. He was converted in 1779 through a fellow apprentice shoemaker, became a dissenter, and was baptized a believer in 1783. After some local preaching, Carey became pastor of Moulton Baptist Chapel (1786), supporting himself through teaching and shoemaking. In 1792 Carey published *An Enquiry into the Obligation of Christians to use Means for the Conversion of the Heathen.* He argued that Christ's great commission to 'preach the gospel to every creature' still applied to all Christians.

In the same year (1792) in a sermon at Nottingham he urged Christians to 'Expect great things!' and 'Attempt great things!' The phrase 'for God' was later added to the quotes because his sermon implied God's role in each. The Baptist Missionary Society was founded soon thereafter as a direct consequence

121

of his stand. As one historian notes, "This was a turning point, marking the entry of the English-speaking world on a large scale into the missionary enterprise - and it has continued to be that the English-speaking world provides four-fifths of the protestant missionaries up till now."

Carey translated the complete Bible into 6 languages, and portions into 29 others, yet he never attended the equivalent of high school or college. At the age of 12 Carey had taught himself Latin. Later, on his own he mastered Greek, Hebrew, French, and Dutch.

Once he landed in India, Carey never once took a furlough in 41 years of service in India. He was married 3 times, and he baptized all three of his wives. The burden of his heart and life was embodied in his statement, "the forming of our native brethren to usefulness, fostering every kind of genius, and cherishing every gift and grace in them; in this respect we can scarcely be too lavish in our attention to their improvement. It is only by means of native preachers we can hope for the universal spread of the Gospel through this immense continent."

4. Truths Restored in the 19th Century

At the end of the 18th Century the 13 Colonies in North America broke free from mother England to become an independent nation. The attention of many men turned from their intense interest in serving Jesus brought about by the Great Awakening to the all-absorbing concern of politics and survival. From 1775 until 1789 the birth of a new nation was the focus of all colonists. Religiously speaking the event of greatest significance was the freedom of religion that America was incorporating into the very fiber of their government. At the turn of the century the greatest activity regarding the Restoration of Truth was back in England.

a. The Evangelicals

Three groups emerged from the Evangelical Revival of the 18th Century, the *Methodists*, separated from the Church of England after Wesley's death; the *Calvinists*, successors of Whitefield; and the *Evangelical Anglicans*, of whom the key figures were Samuel Walker of Truro, Henry Venn of Huddersfield and John Newton of Olney.

The Methodists continued to emphasize that Christ died for all men, and that some might attain Christian perfection in this life. The Calvinists believed that Christ died only for the elect, and stressed that human nature was fallen in every aspect. The Anglican Evangelicals believed that Christ died for the whole world; they also believed in total depravity, and shared with both the other groups that their sins were forgiven. They also held that, through Christian Missions, the whole world would eventually come to faith in Christ. They broke with the main body of Reformers when they determined that at the end Christ would return and then the millennium would begin. This last group became known as the Clapham Sect, which became the founders of the Church Missionary Society, the British and Foreign Bible Society and the Religious Tract Society.

Wesley had begun a revolution in morals and behavior among the working classes. This revolution spread to other classes at the beginning of the 19th Century through the writings of William Wilberforce and his friend, Hannah More. She wrote simple moral tales, in homely English. Her tracts were distributed door-to-door. They were circulated in huge numbers, being read even among the upper classes. For the privileged classes Wilberforce wrote his book, *A Practical View of the Prevailing Religious System of Professed Christians in the Higher and Middle Classes in this Country Contrasted with Real Christianity.*

In his book Wilberforce commented on the increase of prosperity, the growth of the new cities, the splendor and luxury of the age, and the decline of religion, manners and morals. He reminded the rich of their duties to the poor, and claimed that the only remedy for the selfishness that their wealth encouraged was to turn from their nominal Christianity to the real Christianity to be found in a true personal commitment to Jesus Christ as their Savior. 7,500 copies were sold in 6 months. Few religious books have ever been more influential.

The 'reformation of manners' for which Wilberforce campaigned took place before his very eyes. Cock fighting, bull- and bear-baiting died out through lack of support. Bookshops selling 'dirty books' had to close down for lack of customers. In fact, within the first 20 years of the 19th Century a complete change came over the social habits of Britain, as they became 'Victorian' in their life-styles.

In Eerdman's *Handbook to the History of Christianity* (pp.512-514) Evangelical ranks continued to divide in the 1820's, as Edward Irving began to disrupt the ranks with his end-time doctrines. He convinced many evangelicals that they were far too optimistic about the conversion of the world; in fact, the day of judgment was at hand. He initiated the belief that Christ's second coming would precede the millennium. He believed that the missionary societies were deceiving the elect by talking of the conversion of the world.

b. Brethren

The term, **Brethren**, is used in the designation of various Protestant sects. There is a variety of groups that use this designation; the Bohemian Brethren; Dunkers, or the Church of the Brethren; the Evangelical United Brethren Church; the Moravian Brethren or Herrnhuters; the Exclusive Brethren or Darbyites, also known as the Plymouth Brethren; and the United Brethren in Christ.

This movement emphasized the sufficiency of the Bible for every need in life and in the ordering of the affairs of the Church. They also believed in the truth that the Body of Christ is really just ONE body. They also believed that every believer was in the New Testament priesthood. This movement, unlike many before, embraced to a large extent much of what had previously been revealed to the Church as they strove to recapture the outlook and beliefs of the Church of the New Testament. This group was rooted in the Anglican Evangelicals, but resisted labeling themselves in any unique way as a whole.

From the start there were two different emphases. J.N. Darby and others believed that the Church was in ruins, as at the end of other "dispensations" of God's dealings with men. The assemblies were not to be set up with elders and deacons, but simply to be groups of people separated from the world awaiting Christ's any moment return. Later theses 'exclusive' assemblies declined into authoritarianism.

The other grouping, simply known as Christian Brethren (or 'open' Brethren), developed into a small but influential nonconformist group. This group had such a strong emphasis on missions that they spread to all parts of the world. Their most distinctive emphasis was, and is, that the ministry and gifts of the Holy Spirit are to be distributed to all believers. The communion service is to be led by different members of the congregation. Full-time pastors are rare, but their full-time Evangelists and Bible Teachers still travel widely.

124

Dispensationalism - This system of belief breaks down the history of the Bible into 7 distinct groups, called dispensations. Birthed by Edward Irving and nurtured by J. N. Darby, these beliefs were formalized by C. I. Schofield. With these dispensations comes the concepts of; a secret rapture of the Church, a distinction between Israel and the Church, the GAP or postponement theory of Daniel's 70 Week Prophecy, and several other innovations.

SCOFIELD'S Seven Dispensations-

(1) Innocence - Gen. 1:28

(2) Conscience - Gen. 3:7 - or Moral Responsibility

(3) Human Government - Gen. 3:15

(4) Promise - Gen. 21:1

(5) Law - Ex. 19:1

(6) Church - Acts 2:1 - or 'Of the Spirit' - here is his GAP

(7) Kingdom - Rev. 20:4 - the Millennium on Earth

EIGHT BIBLICAL COVENANTS – which now are widely accepted in contrast to Dispensations.

(1) Edenic - Gen. 1:26-30

(2) Adamic - Gen. 3:14-19

(3) Noahic - Gen. 8:20-9:17

(4) Abrahamic - Gen. 12

(5) Mosaic - Deut. 4:13

(6) Israelic or Palestinian - Deut. 29 & 30

(7) Davidic - 2 Sam. 6:13-15

(8) New or Everlasting - Heb. 13:20

c. **The Holiness Movement**

According to the Encarta Encyclopedia this movement involved fundamental Protestant bodies that developed from Methodism and held as their distinguishing feature the doctrine that holiness, or sanctification of the individual, occurs by a second act of grace that follows justification and is supplementary to it. The experience of holiness is also referred to as the second blessing. The National Holiness Movement came into being shortly after the American Civil War. Originally a protest movement within Methodism, it opposed those Methodists that fell away from the emphasis on sanctification that John Wesley, the founder of Methodism, had developed. He had stressed original sin and justification by faith and added that the individual may be assured of forgiveness by a direct experience of the spirit, called sanctification, which he regarded as the step leading to Christian perfection.

The major representatives of the Holiness movement (excluding Pentecostal denominations) are the Church of the Nazarene, the Church of God (Anderson, Indiana) and later the Christian Missionary Alliance. The latter originated about 1880 as a movement within existing churches to promote Christian unity. The founders were interested in relieving the church at large of what they believed was over-ecclesiasticism and restrictive organization and in reaffirming the New Testament as the true standard of faith and life. In addition to the holiness principle, they believe in, among other doctrines, the divine inspiration of the Scriptures, forgiveness of sin through the death of Christ and the repentance of the sinner, an Amillennial concept of the return of Christ, and external reward or punishment as a result of the final judgment.

Albert Benjamin Simpson (1844-1919) – According to Dick Iverson he was better known as A.B. Simpson, was originally ordained a Presbyterian minister in 1865 and ministered for about 10 years. He then experienced a profound renewal of relationship with his living Savior. He came into what he termed the "fullness of the blessing of Christ", or sanctification "through faith in the provision of the atonement." Whatever his experience, it revolutionized his Christian life.

With his tremendous zeal for the Lord, he soon overworked himself, and his health gave out completely. It was during this time that he searched the Scriptures in regard to the nature of man, the nature of sin, and our position as believers in Christ. He saw man as consisting of a two-fold nature. He saw him as being both a material and a spiritual being. Both natures had been equally affected by the fall, His body was exposed to disease; his soul was corrupted by sin. The more he studied, the more he believed that God had made provision for the sin-sick soul AND for the sicknesses and diseases relating to the body. God confirmed this word to him by healing

126

him and extending his ministry another 35 years. God was restoring the truth of divine healing to the Church.

Simpson preached and wrote about what God had shown him. He had tremendous success in his healing campaigns, and eventually founded the Christian Missionary Alliance. He proclaimed what he called the "four-fold Gospel" - Jesus Christ as Savior, Sanctifier, Healer and Coming King. The following are some principles of divine healing that are taken from his book, *The Gospel of Healing*.

a. The causes of disease and suffering are distinctly traced to the fall and sinful nature of man.

b. If disease is the result of the fall, then we may expect it to be embraced in the provision of Redemption.

c. In Christ's life on earth we see a complete vision of what Christianity should be, and from His Words and works we may gather the full plan of redemption.

d. But redemption finds its center in the Cross of our Lord Jesus Christ, and there we must look for the fundamental principles of divine healing.

e. The death of Christ destroyed sin, the root of sickness, but it is the life of Christ (based on His resurrection) that is the source of health and life.

f. This new life must come, like all the blessings of Christ's redemption, as the free grace of God, without works, and without distinction of merit or respect of persons.

g. The simple condition of this great blessing is faith without sight. As with Abraham, an act of faith is required to appropriate the gift.

5. Truths Restored in the 20ᵗʰ Century

A few short years after the restoration of the truth of divine healing through the ministry of A.B. Simpson, God started moving in mighty ways all over the earth. Sincere Christians everywhere began fasting and praying, seeking God for further visitations. In 1904-05 the Welsh Revival broke out. This seems to have been a real spark for something that had already been smoldering in America. For several years there had been urgency among many of God's people that God was about to move. God confirmed these feelings by a sporadic outpouring of the Spirit. In 1896 in a small group in North Carolina, God opened heaven's windows and poured out of His Spirit, and men began to prophesy and speak with other tongues. In 1901 God did the same thing to a group of believers in Topeka, Kansas, setting the stage for a great outpouring a few years later.

In 1906 in Los Angeles during the now famous Azusa Street revivals, God poured out of His Spirit in a miraculous way. As Frederick Bruner puts it, "At the Azusa Street meetings the Pentecostal movement ignited. Its fires were apparently so intense that they were felt within a short time around the world. The conflagration swept first across America itself."

a. The Pentecostal Movement

Harvey Cox, Victor Thomas Professor of Religion at Harvard University, is the author of *Fire from Heaven*. In this book he chronicles the rise of Pentecostal spirituality and the reshaping of religion in the twentieth century. The following is his description of the beginning of the Pentecostal Movement.

The epic of how the Pentecostal crusade continued to grow until it encircled the globe includes many players. But it is impossible to understand Pentecostalism's origins without reference to the story of one particular man. *William Joseph Seymour*, a black preacher born in 1870 of parents whose were former slaves in Centreville, Louisiana, had an inclination to the "Holiness" teachings about the indwelling Christ that were then sweeping the south. With no formal education, he had taught himself to read. But nothing in Seymour's early life would make him the natural choice of a Hollywood casting office for the role of social visionary. From the outset Seymour was restless, a man on the move. In his twenties he left Louisiana for Indianapolis where he worked as a waiter in a fancy hotel and attended the local Methodist Episcopal Church.

By the time he was thirty, Seymour had moved on to Cincinnati. Somewhere along the line he had been "saved and sanctified" by a revivalist group called the Evening Light Saints. These believers taught that human history was approaching its dusk and that Christ would appear soon to set up His Kingdom, but that before the final denouement, God would shower fresh gifts of the Spirit on the faithful. Just as a "latter rain" would fall on the spiritually parched earth, so also a bright light would illuminate the gathering darkness.

Seymour soon moved from Cincinnati to Houston,

128

where he attended a black church in which he witnessed something he had never encountered before. He heard a woman pray aloud in a language, or in what seemed to be a language that no one there could understand. Seymour was touched to the core. As a man of prayer himself, he could sense that this woman had somehow attained a depth of spiritual intensity he had long sought but never found. But he was also excited because in the popular Holiness theology of the day such "speaking in tongues" was held to be a sure sign of the imminent coming of the Last Days and the descent of the heavenly city foreseen in Revelation.

These experiences changed Seymour's life. After the meeting he asked *Lucy Farrow*, the woman who had spoken in the strange tongue, more about her remarkable gift. In response she introduced him to *Charles Fox Parham*, a white preacher who ran a Holiness school in the same city, and for whom she had once worked as a governess in Topeka, Kansas. Eagerly, Seymour sought out Parham and begged to be admitted to the school. Parham hesitated. A Ku Klux Klan sympathizer, he did not feel ready to welcome this obviously earnest, but just as obviously black, seeker. On the other hand, to turn him away completely would seem uncharitable. So Parham compromised. He told Seymour he could listen to the lectures seated on a chair outside an open window. On rainy days he was permitted to sit inside the building, but in the hallway outside the classroom, with the door left ajar.

Seymour was not discouraged. He listened through the window and prayed ardently for the new baptism of the Spirit and the gift of tongues. But strive as he would for his own "personal Pentecost," the experience somehow eluded him. Eventually his preaching and testifying drew the interest of *Julia Hutchins*, a preacher in Los Angeles, who invited Seymour to come and assist her in her labors. Seymour considered this a "Macedonian call" and immediately set out for Los Angeles. He came to preach about the New Jerusalem and the renewed experience of Pentecost that had now become available to all who would hear and believe.

Shortly after his arrival Seymour preached his first sermon at Sister Hutchin's storefront church on Santa Fe Avenue. He was not a great success.

As a matter of fact, they not only disagreed with his

theology, but one day he arrived for an afternoon prayer meeting only to find the doors locked. Faced with a bolted door, Seymour did what thousands of Pentecostal preachers have done in similar circumstances ever since. He carried on. With no money even to rent a storefront, he began organizing prayer meetings in the humble homes of black friends and sympathizers. The street on which one of these house worship meetings took place was **Bonnie Brae Avenue**, in a neighborhood that had fallen into straitened circumstances. Seymour's congregation at first consisted largely of black domestic servants and washerwomen.

Seymour, it seems, lit the fire. Visitors - black and white - from Nazarene, Holiness, Baptist, and other congregations began to find their way to the little house of Brother and Sister Asberry at 214 North Bonnie Brae Avenue. They listened and prayed, and when they returned they brought their friends and neighbors. But still, no one had yet spoken in tongues. Then, on *April 9, 1906*, as Seymour was preparing to go to the meeting, the friend at whose house he was staying, *Edward Lee*, a black janitor, told him about a vision he had experienced. The Apostles, it seemed, had come to him and told him how to reclaim the gift of tongues. Both men prayed, and that night, in the modest house on North Bonnie Brae Avenue, according to Pentecostal sacred history, the "power fell." Several participants began praising God in unknown tongues, and among these was William Seymour himself.

Now there was no keeping the crowds away. Some came to seek the new power, some to chuckle, others to satisfy their curiosity. Frequently the visitors were so numerous they could not fit into the house, so Seymour began preaching from the porch. More came, and it became evident that enlarged quarters were needed. Acting quickly, Seymour's friends located a vacant two-story, white-washed, wooden frame building at *312 Azusa Street* that had most recently been used as a stable. It smelled of horses and had neither pews nor a pulpit, but Seymour and his friends seized the day. They rented it, cleaned it, placed timbers on upended nail kegs for benches, and piled up empty shoeboxes for a pulpit. On April 14, the first service was held.

Within days the word was out all over Los Angeles. Something was happening in the little church in the colored section of town. There is a favorite saying among Pentecostalists: "The man with an experience is never at the mercy of the man with a doctrine." And on Azusa Street, people were experiencing what they had never experienced before. The outer forms of worship themselves were not all that different from what one might have found in any Nazarene or Holiness church. There were songs and testimonies, spontaneous sermons and exhortations, joyous shouts and prayers punctuated by sobs and tears. There were intercessions for the sick. Even the fact that people sang and spoke in an idiom that sounded like foreign languages, though unusual at the time, was not entirely new.

The Azusa Street revival itself continued day after day, month after month for three years. The janitors and washerwomen who huddled in the converted stable in Los Angeles believed that they stood on the edge of a new era. They also believed God was distressed with the disunity and confusion that plagued their religion. They sensed that what was happening among them was like a new Pentecost, a mighty gathering together of the tribes and nations that had been scattered and confounded at the foot of the ill-fated Tower of Babel. They saw signs and omens of this new dispensation everywhere. But they also sensed that when the flames came, they would purge and purify as well as enliven and inspire.

The people who first met at Azusa Street were usually minorities and from the wrong side of the tracks. Eventually, though, even white people began to crowd into the Azusa Street revival - but these, too, were mainly unlettered, unrefined, and, as often as not, unemployed as well. Even when the fire fell, and when the embers began to waft across the country, and then across the seas, the scoffers continued to scorn. These "holy rollers" were either demented or demonic, or they were comical or scandalous, or they were all of these at once. What kind of a God would entrust a revival of religion to such people?

But despite ridicule and opposition, the conflagration continued to expand as the sparks blew from ghetto to slum to rural hamlet, to St. Louis and New York, and then across the oceans to Europe and Asia, Africa and South America.

b. The 1948 Revival

Returning to Pastor Dick Iverson's book on Present Day Truths, he picks up the story this way.

131

As we move on from the early 1900's, we find that God has opened the doors of further truth, leading us a step further in His wonderful plan. In the late 1940's there was a renewed soberness among many Christians in conservative circles. They still felt that they had not experienced all that God had for them. They had experienced salvation by faith; they had been baptized; they were filled with the Spirit; but they still had a longing in their heart for more of God. They knew that there had to be more to the Christian walk than just getting filled with the Spirit. In several places in different parts of the world there went forth, as it were, the sound of a trumpet calling men together to a solemn assembly (Numbers 10). Men responded to the wooing of the Spirit by gathering themselves together in fasting, prayer and seeking the face of God. Prayer waters revival and visitation.

As men waited before the Lord, there was a sovereign outpouring of the Spirit on some of these that were waiting before Him. Men began to arise and prophesy with a powerful anointing of the Spirit. They prophesied about things that were contrary to their own doctrinal beliefs. They prophesied about the five ascension gift ministries, a further unfolding of the gifts of the Spirit and truths regarding body ministry; but the most pronounced message was in connection with the Laying on of Hands.

These doctrines were new to their experience. They formerly believed none of these things, so they were forced to look to the Word of God. Ultimately the Word must be the final test of any and every doctrine. After discovering in the Word the basis for what had been prophesied, these men began to move in the areas that had been indicated by the Spirit. As they met together, the Spirit continued to flow and open more areas of truth. The Presence of the Lord was so real that no human leader was needed in the services, and yet there was tremendous order. As men entered into God's Presence, audible praise began to flow from their lips in such a way as none had ever experienced.

As God by His Spirit opened some powerful doors to these men, stern warnings came forth in prophecy. God indicated that they were only to operate in these realms as the Spirit directed. If they disobeyed, the move would go into religious chaos. This is precisely what happened. Although not everyone who was involved in this visitation disobeyed, many of those who were involved abused and misused the gifts that God gave them. Those groups indeed ended in chaos. The truths were right, but men corrupted them. Some, though, heeded the warnings and preserved the truths that God had revealed to them.

The central truth that was unlocked in this visitation was the laying on of hands. But, as men pursued after the hidden treasures in the Word of God with a renewed zeal, God began to unfold more and more of His ultimate purpose. Some of these truths include the following:

(1) The Restoration of the Lost Years.   (*Joel 2:25*)

(2) The Restoration of Full Fruit and the Gifts of the Spirit.

(3) The Laying on of Hands.   (*Heb. 6:2*)

(4) The Revelation of the Body of Christ. (*John 17:20-22*)

(5) The Five Ascension Gift Ministries. (*Eph. 4:11-12*)

(6) The Principles of Church Order and Government.

(7) Worship in Spirit and Truth. (*John 4:23-24*)

(8) The Tabernacle of David.   (*Acts 15:15-18*)

(9) The Seven Principles of the Doctrine of Christ. (*Heb. 6:1-2*)

(10) The Maturity of the Saints. (*Eph. 4:14-16*)

All former visitations dealt chiefly with the relation of the believer to God as an individual. They included an emphasis on man's personal salvation, his personal death and burial in baptism, his personal walk, his personal health and his personal reception of the Holy Spirit. This move, however, is on a different level. The areas that have been illuminated by the Spirit in the present move all have to do with the corporate Body of Christ. The trumpet call that sounded was a call for the gathering together of the Body - a call to oneness or spiritual unity. It is this Body or Man which God is building or fashioning that is to be conformed to the IMAGE. It is this many-membered man (*I Cor. 12*).

There is something more for the People of God. Many would tend to get lax in spiritual matters waiting for the coming of the Lord. We believe with men of God around the world that we are living in the glorious climax of the Ages. What can we expect? What is our part and responsibility at the end of the Age? Are we just to wait for a secret rapture to take us all away? Will the Church grow weaker and smaller until there is just God's "little flock" left? NO! Absolutely not! For nearly five hundred years the Lord has been bringing back (restoring) truth to the Church, and He continues to do so even in the present day. Certainly any believer with spiritual eyes can see that we have been in the process of receiving truth, line upon line and precept upon precept. And for what purpose? Is it because God is having fun with us? NO! God is doing all of this that He might present to His Son a glorious (glory-us) bride without spot or wrinkle (*Eph. 5:27*).

c. Revivals and Movements from 1950 to 2000's

While hindsight is reported to be 20-20, it does seem apparent that sometimes we are so close to the forest that we can't see the trees. In other words, it is sometimes very difficult to assess the historical value of current events. In the last 60 years it seems that what God has been doing has been to further illuminate the revelations given during the 1948 Revival. As we begin to look at what God has been doing during this period, I realize that my perspective might be limited. I have tried to draw upon my personal experience as well as what others have written and experienced. What I do notice is that it seems very little new truth has been revealed to the body at large. Instead I see that each movement or revival has more or less simply amplified the truths that were restored in 1948.

1950's

Revivalists - During this era the large outdoor, or tent, evangelistic revival services became popular. Tommy Hicks, T.L. Osborn, Joseph Mattsson-Boze, Leroy Jenkins, Oral Roberts, William Branham, Billy Graham and Rex Humbard among many others rode the wave of this movement. Great numbers of people were affected by the crusades. Salvations and Divine Healings seemed to be the main emphasis. These meetings would sometimes last weeks, with several meetings per day. (*Excesses* at times seemed to be the problem with this movement.)

1960's

Charismatic Renewal - This widespread move of the Holy Spirit involved the mainline churches and their acceptance of the Gifts of the Holy Spirit. Father

Dennis Bennet in Seattle, David DuPlessis and Demos Shakarian are names of note that God used mightily. Crossing all denominational barriers, speaking in tongues and the renewed use of the gifts of the Holy Spirit became an accepted part of many church liturgies. Often as not a separate service was started to facilitate the use of the gifts. Prayer for the sick, anointing with oil, and expressive worship services were the hallmarks of the renewal. (*Greasy Grace* was the criticism of this renewal.)

Jesus People Movement - A phenomenon that essentially began in Southern California as those in the Hippie Movement began to turn to Christ. It was God's answer to the cry of young people desperately searching for love and peace. Calvary Chapel under the ministry of Chuck Smith revolutionized the way the church looked at, preached to, accepted and assimilated the youth involved in the drug, sex, and hippie culture. Nothing short of a revolution in music took place as the likes of Barry McGuire, Terry Clark, Keith Green, Annie Herring, Jamie Owens Collins, Chuck Girard, the Love Song and the Second Chapter of Acts began composing and performing songs and sounds birthed by the Holy Spirit. (*Sloppy Agape* was the criticism of this movement.)

1970's

Discipleship Movement - As young people by the thousands came into the kingdom of God the need for their growth and development became apparent. The Holy Spirit began to blow upon the scriptures dealing with discipleship and growth. Juan Carlos Ortiz from Argentina spearheaded this movement based on extreme submission to spiritual leaders. Total commitment was the watchword of the day. (*"Submit or split"* was how this move eventually was categorized.)

Bible Colleges - All across the United States and throughout the world God began to birth training institutes to further develop the Joshua Generation. Elim Bible Institute, Christ for the Nations, Oral Roberts University, Portland Bible College, the YWAM group, Berean Bible College and a host of others came on the scene during this time. (*Zeal without knowledge* was the all too applicable critique.)

Covenant Movement - Bob Mumford, Ern Baxter and Derek Prince among others gave fresh impetus to the

Teaching Ministry as they taught on covenantal relationships. This movement built on the Discipleship Movement but added to it the need for interpersonal relationships and accountability. (*Demons* and *authoritarianism* were the problems in this move.)

Faith Movement - The power of your confession, or the word of faith, were the hallmarks of this movement. Kenneth Hagin, Kenneth Copeland and Jerry Seville led the charge with their teaching and preaching on the power of your words. (*Name it and claim it* showed the extreme this move gravitated towards.)

1980's

Church Growth Movement - Again crossing denominational barriers, large Churches developed in step with the seminars, books and teachings about church growth. Yongi Cho, Lyle Schaller, Robert Schuller, and C. Peter Wagner continue to present principles upon which congregations can leap to the next level of numerical growth. (The *numbers game* is a frequent critique here.)

Cell Groups - As churches began growing the need for intimacy with other believers became apparent. Care groups or cell groups met the need. Lyle Coleman, Denny Ryberg, Richard Peace and Gary Christopherson designed materials under the name of Serendipity that helped get small groups together, study the Bible and become a caring community. Large churches immediately saw the benefit of creating the small church feeling while enjoying the large church benefits. (*Renegade leaders* gathering people unto themselves was the danger here.)

1990 - 2000's

The Renewal - Out of the Vineyard Movement, originally led by John Wimber, came the 'Toronto Blessing' (from which the Vineyard Movement subsequently disassociated themselves). Pastor John Arnott of the Toronto Vineyard encouraged unusual manifestations such as laughing, weeping, dancing, being 'slain in the spirit', barking, roaring and other animal noises as a part of the renewal. Later, many testified to a deep spirit of repentance that moved upon the participants as God dealt with them during their "carpet time". It spread to Pensacola, Florida and then to many parts of the globe. The hallmark of this move is not so much the revelation of scripture

136

as it is an emphasis on emotional demonstrations and experiences. Many new choruses are also being birthed in this move pertaining to the renewal.

Unity - Something quite remarkable has quietly been taking place that is restoring the unity of the body. Jesus prayed in John 17 that His body would be one body. A current move of God is seeing Christians from all spectrums coming together in different venues in a united attempt to extend the Kingdom of God.

Promise Keepers - is a men's group that focuses on a man's commitment to Christ, his family and his church. Literally reaching across all denominational and movement barriers, this movement has gathered thousands of men in large stadiums and coliseums for teaching and worship services.

Women of Faith - is doing much the same, yet for women. They also use the stadium and large conference approach, as well as using the teaching and worship services.

Pastor's Fellowships - Like never before there is a grass roots movement among Pastors in communities to come together in Christ. In 1994 many prominent Catholics and Evangelical-Protestants came together and created a document highlighting their similarities in doctrine and liturgy - but at the same time addressing in a theological manner their differences. In 1995 Ted Haggard wrote a book, *Primary Purpose*, which has done much to help Pastors focus on what they agree on, rather than on the divisive rhetoric that has kept many from fellowship in the past. One of the focus events has been the March for Jesus rallies that take place annually now in June across the nation and around the world.

Reaching The World - Like never before Churches and parachurch organizations alike are seriously pursuing spreading the Gospel to the entire world. Much of the mission activity today is among the third world nations - recruiting, sending and supporting their own missionaries throughout the world. The *Joshua Project* shares statistics on their website that track how many unreached people groups are still left.

Worship - With the help of hi-tech advances and the Internet, worship has exploded throughout the spectrum of the Church. Integrity-Hosanna, Marantha, Vineyard and Hillsong music has revolutionized worship through the spread of new songs and styles of worship.

Conclusion

Where are we today, and where are we going? I trust that with me, you sense a need to be a part of what God is constantly doing in the Church.

John Robinson said in his farewell address to the Pilgrim fathers on their departure from England on the Mayflower; "If God reveals anything to you by another instrument, be as ready to receive it as ever you were to receive any truth by my ministry, for I am persuaded that the Lord has more truth yet to break forth out of His Holy Word."

God is a God of progressive revelation of His Word. Let's never put a period after what we believe He has revealed to us. As we see what God has done in the past it is obvious that not one group or movement has recovered everything or finished this process of restoration. Let's treat like some communicable disease the attitude that we might have a corner on what God has revealed, or that we might have it all. This has been a trap that many have fallen into in the past. Spiritual pride of this sort has always halted what God was doing within that group. We look at the process of restoration as a divinely instituted plan that must go on until the last day when Jesus returns.

FINAL WORD

My hope and prayer is that this workbook will help develop leaders around the world for years to come. Character, conduct and content, were the topics that I covered in this book as I feel strongly that these are the three areas that must developed in every leader. While not every leader will have the opportunity to take formal classes at a Bible College or University, I trust that what has been compiled here will be effective in the training and development of leaders in local churches within every people group, nation, kindred and tribe.

Enjoying the adventure of extending His kingdom,

Steve Fitzpatrick

ABOUT THE AUTHOR STEVE FITZPATRICK

Reverend Steve Fitzpatrick: Pastor, Evangelist and Teacher is currently the President of Herald of Faith. He and his wife Kathy have three children – Jason, Scott and Katelyn, two daughters-in-law – Taylor and Olivia and five grandchildren.

Steve's list of experiences over his 45 years in ministry include; Youth Pastor, Choir Director and Worship Leader, Minister of Evangelism, Evangelist, Assistant Pastor at three different churches, a Senior Pastor, and a Teacher at and Dean of four Bible Colleges. Steve has an Associates of Theology degree from Berean Bible College, a Bachelor of Theology and Masters of Divinity from Azusa Pacific University's Haggard School of Theology.

During his travels he has trained and equipped pastors and leaders on six continents while visiting over forty countries, frequently visiting the same country up to 25 times.

BIBLIOGRAPHY

Augustine of Hippo. *The City of God*. London: Penguin Classics, Reprint 2004.

Barnes, Albert. *Barnes' Notes*. Grand Rapids: Zondervan Publishing, 1983.

Beall, James L. *Laying the Foundation*. Plainfield NJ: Logos International, 1976.

Bevere, John. *Under Cover*. Nashville: Thomas Nelson Publishing, 2001.

Bock, Darrell L. *Three Views on the Millennium and Beyond*. Grand Rapids: Zondervan Publishing House, 1999.

Bush, L. Russ. *Classical Readings in Christian Apologetics*. Grand Rapids: Zondervan, 1983.

Chambers, Oswald. *My Utmost for His Highest*. Grand Rapids: Discovery House Publishers, 1992.

Cox, Harvey. *Fire From Heaven*. Boston: Da Capo Press, 1995.

Cox, William E. *Amillennialism Today*. Phillipsburg NJ: P & R Publishing, 1966.

Cox, William E. *Biblical Studies in Final Things*. Phillipsburg NJ: P & R Publishing, 1966.

Damazio, Frank. *The Making of a Leader*. Portland: City Bible Publishing, 1988.

Davids, Peter H. *The First Epistle of Peter*. Grand Rapids: W. B Eerdmans Publishing, 1990.

Dowley, Tim, ed. *Eerdman's Handbook to the History of Christianity*. Grand Rapids: Eerdman's Publishing, 1977.

Garlock, John. *Keys to Better Preaching*. Broken Arrow OK: Faith Library Publications, 2014.

Gonzalez, Justo L. *The Story of Christianity*. Peabody: Prince Press, 2004

Halley, Henry H. *Halley's Bible Handbook*, Grand Rapids: Zondervan Publishing, 1965.

Hamilton, Victor P. *Handbook on the Pentateuch*. Grand Rapids: Baker Academic, 2005.

Hendriksen, W. *More Than Conquerors*. Grand Rapids: Baker Book House, 1967.

Henry, Matthew. *Matthew Henry's Commentary on the Whole Bible*. Peabody: Hendrickson Publishers, 2008.

Hoekema, Anthony A. *The Bible and the Future*. Grand Rapids: W. B. Eerdmans Publishing, 1979.

Hughes, Phillip E. *The Book of the Revelation*. Grand Rapids: W. B. Eerdmans Publishing, 1990.

Hybels, Bill. *Who You Are When No One's Looking*. Downers Grove: IVPress, 1987.

Iverson, Dick. *Present Day Truths*. Portland: City Bible Publishing, 1976.

Keller, Phillip. *A Shepherd Looks at Psalms 23*. Grand Rapids: Zondervan Publishing, 2007.

Laymon, Charles M. *The Book of Revelation*. New York: Abingdon Press, 1960.

Lowry, Eugene L. *The Homiletical Plot*. Louisville: Westminster John Know Press, 2001.

Mauro, Phillip. *The Seventy Weeks and the Great Tribulation*. Sterling VA: Grace Abounding Ministries, 1988.

Microsoft Encarta Multimedia Encyclopedia. www.britannica.com, 1998.

Miller, Kevin A., ed. *Christian History Magazine*, 1995.

Miriam Webster Dictionary. Boston: Riverside Publishing, 1984.

Mounce, Robert H. *The Book of Revelation*. Grand Rapids: W. B. Eerdmans Publishing, 1977.

Provan, Charles D. *The Church is Israel Now.* Vallecito Ca: Ross House Books, 1987.

Robertson, A. T. *Word Pictures in the NT*. Electronic E4 Group, 2014.

Robinson, Haddon W. *Biblical Preaching.* Grand Rapids: Baker Academic, 2001.

Smith, Wendell. *Great Faith: Making God Big.* Portland: City Bible Publishing, 2001.

Stott, John. *The Message of 2 Timothy*. Downers Grove: IVPress, 1973.

Stott, John. *The Preacher's Portrait*. Grand Rapids: Wm. B. Eerdmans Publishing, 1961.

Strong's Exhaustive Concordance. Pella: World Bible Publishers.

Vincent, Marvin R. *Word Studies in the NT*. New York: Charles Scriber's Sons, 1887.

Walker, Williston. *History of the Christian Church*. New York: Pearson Publishing, 1985.

Wuest, Kenneth S. *Word Studies from the Greek NT*. Grand Rapids: W. B. Eerdmans Publishing, 1980.

Wycliffe Bible Encyclopedia. Chicago: Moody Press, 1975.

www.ingramcontent.com/pod-product-compliance
Lightning Source LLC
Chambersburg PA
CBHW081543090426
42741CB00013BA/3244